T0113689

This book is deeply touching with the author's raw-honesty regarding a "shattering" struggle in his life. The book brings to focus some of the absolutely maddening short-comings in our mental health field and often hideous obstacles for those in pain that seek help. Pastor Otto's journey provides a startling and compelling alert to people in positions that purport to be helpers. The author delivers his personal story with practical ideas as well as providing uplifting encouragement and hope for those fighting their own overwhelming psychological battles. As a Licensed Psychologist I applaud Pastor Otto's bravery, humility, and humor in the telling of his story. I am delighted to recommend this book.

Julie Diaz, PhD

"In *Finding Myself Again*, Pastor Brad Otto risks sharing his own struggle with mental illness, while unmasking the weaknesses of our mental health care system and challenging the church up its game. His story reminds us how many people suffer in silence, while at the same time offering us hope and a way though."

Michael Rinehart, Bishop of the Gulf Coast Synod, Evangelical Lutheran Church in America

Rev. Brad Otto has written a profoundly moving, insightful, and personal story about his mental health crisis and his journey of recovery and healing. It will touch your life and the lives of all who struggle with mental health issues. Otto is bold and yet vulnerable in telling his story of a mental collapse that led to an honest self-assessment of his values and life commitments. He writes in a way that captures the intensity of the struggle that many keep hidden and locked up for fear of shame and rejection. This is a book about a pastor and his family who journeys together on a road to recovery and healing. Their story should be read by every mental health counsellor and every church leader who seeks the wellness of their pastor, family and community.

Rev. Javier (Jay) Alanís, PhD, JD

"In his memoir, Reverend Otto gets to the heart of the struggles challenging the millions who suffer from one of the many forms of mental illness.... He documents the challenges of getting help, discerning what form of help would actually help, and the embarrassment of having to set aside his hopes for himself, his family, and his congregation to delve into the confusing and frustrating world of mental health programs and resources."

Rev. Kathryn Haueisen

"In our modern socio-political climate, in which many are desperately seeking authenticity from the Church and its leaders, this book is a breath of fresh air. Far too often, we're afraid to be honest about who we really are. We're afraid to be human. But the truth is that real people -- yes, even pastors -- struggle with depression, anxiety, loneliness, fear, and doubt. In candidly sharing his story, Brad offers a dose of real authenticity and hope to seekers everywhere who need to know they're not alone."

Joshua Darwin, Author

Finding
Myself
Again

*My Struggle
With Mental Health and
Finding Peace Again*

B R A D   O T T O

Archway Publishing books may be ordered through booksellers or by contacting:

Archway Publishing
1663 Liberty Drive
Bloomington, IN 47403
www.archwaypublishing.com
844-669-3957

ISBN: 978-1-6657-3063-1 (sc)
ISBN: 978-1-6657-3064-8 (e)

Library of Congress Control Number: 2022917602

Print information available on the last page.

Archway Publishing rev. date: 10/10/2022

Contents

Foreword

The Rev. Br. Chris Markert, OLF
Bishop's Associate for Mission
Evangelical Lutheran Church in America

In 2003 I was diagnosed with general anxiety disorder. I thought I was having a heart attack since I felt like I couldn't catch my breath. This led me to the ER where I learned it was actually a massive panic attack. I ultimately made it to a cardiologist and, after several medical tests and tons of blood work, I was relieved to hear that my heart was strong and my blood pressure was good. After delivering this good news, she suggested that I may have generalized anxiety and asked a simple question: "How would you rate the stress in your life?" With that question, I crumpled onto the exam table with deep sobs that lasted several minutes. Bingo! We had a winner!

Over the years I've been fortunate in my experiences navigating doctors, medications, and insurance. Early in my ministry, I was protective about sharing my struggles with anxiety. When I finally chose to make myself vulnerable with the churches I served as pastor, I felt supported and encouraged.

I currently serving in a regional denominational office where my bishop and colleagues continue to support me, even if they may not personally know the ins and outs of my experiences. I have used my personal experience with mental health issues as I accompany pastors, deacons, and lay leaders in their ministries today. I am what Carl Jung calls a "wounded healer."

I have known Pastor Brad Otto for nearly 20 years as a great friend and close colleague. His story and experience with mental

health differs from mine. He writes boldly about the realization of his mental health struggles, their effects on his family, his physical and spiritual health, and his ministry as a pastor.

This book tells his story, his truth. Through his story, Brad creates an invitation for you, the reader, to better understand mental health issues for yourself and others. His story also challenges the church to do better, to provide resources and care to pastors, deacons, and people of the church who may struggle with mental illness. Brad, too, is a wounded healer.

Listen to Brad's important words of reality and hope, not just for the Church but for the world. Remember, you don't need to be ashamed of any struggles with mental health and there is help if you need it. May this book be a blessing to you.

Acknowledgments

Where do I even begin? It's a long list, and I will probably leave some folks out, but here are a few big shout-outs I would like to give:

The Staff and Leadership at Messiah Lutheran Cypress: You were there for me through it all. You continued for me when I couldn't go on. You made sure I took care of myself first and didn't have to worry about what was happening at the church. As a result, not many people knew what was really going on. You simply amaze me and I am fortunate to serve in ministry with you all.

Rev. Dr. Javier Alanis: You are my mentor and are always there when I am dealing with a faith crisis. As I wrote my story, you helped guide me and offered insights that I hadn't thought of myself. You are forever *mi hermano*. Muchas gracias!

Josh Darwin: You helped make the gibberish I was writing readable! I am forever grateful to you for helping me put all of this together into a cohesive and relatable story. Your editing skills are unmatched and I wouldn't be at this place without your guidance along the way. Thank you!

Nora and Wayne (Mom and Dad): You have been there for me since I took my first breath. You have always provided for me and have been there for me through the ups and downs. You never flinched. You are the best parents a guy could ask for and I love you both immensely.

Stacie: Last but certainly not least, my wife, my rock, and my heart. You took our wedding vows to the extreme when you promised "in good times and in bad, for better or for worse" and I am ever so grateful to have you in my life. You and the kids got me through the darkest moments of my life. You never wavered and you kept me going. This was just as hard for you as it was for me and yet we made it through. Thank you for being a friend. Your heart is true; you are my confidant. Thank you for allowing me to tell our story. I know it's hard for you, but I know you realize that if this helps just one person, it will have been worth it. I love you with every fiber of my being.

Author's Introduction

Even when the dark comes crashing through
When you need a friend to carry you
And when you're broken on the ground
You will be found
So let the sun come streaming in
'Cause you'll reach up and you'll rise again
Lift your head and look around
You will be found[1]

Those words rang especially true for me for about two-and-a-half years when I struggled with mental health. I say struggled, but the truth is that it's a daily struggle that never goes away. It's always there. Sometimes it creeps up its ugly head and that's okay.

How will you deal with your mental health? That's the real question. Destructive thoughts will occur but it's your emotional reaction and your response to those thoughts that ultimately matters.

This book is about my struggle with mental health. From the first time I began to realize that something was wrong, to the two-and-a-half years of struggling to find out what was *really* wrong, to finding my true self again. In a way, *this* is part of my therapy. *You* are a part of my therapy.

Didn't realize that when you picked this book up, did you? One thing I have learned on this journey is that mental health may be a part of you, but it doesn't have to define you. This is

---

[1] Pasek, Benj, and Justin Paul. *Dear Evan Hansen*. Theatre Communications Group, 2017.

the primary truth I came to grips with since it's so easy to *let* it define you.

That particular realization was difficult for me since I'm a Lutheran pastor. Many of us who have been called to ministry feel the need to fit a certain persona. We think we have to have it all together and mental illness doesn't seem to align with that paradigm so we lock it deep inside.

We put on our weekly show from the pulpit, hoping no one notices our pain. Honestly, I believe that's the case with *everyone* who deals with mental health. We can't *see* our mental health and so we often let our issues pass us by. And because people around us can't see it either, we sort of have an excuse not to deal with it.

So I put it off. I thought it would get better; it didn't. What I *really* needed to do was put the same effort into my mental health that I was putting into my physical health. That thought never occurred to me.

My story includes some very intimate details and that's *scary*. Honestly, I'm not proud of some of the things I said or did, but here's the thing: we don't have to be proud of our stories but we do have to *own* them.

I will tell you how I felt the Church (the entire body as a whole) let me down. I'm sure this will not be easy for some to hear and, to be perfectly blunt, I thought long and hard about whether to share that part of my journey. But if I want the Church to change its perception of mental health toward its clergy, then I *must* tell that story. While we might say all the right words, in reality, we have a *very* long way to go. (Names have been changed to protect the identities of those mentioned in this book.)

I'm sure that I'll be criticized and maybe even mocked, but that's okay. In the summer of 2020, gold medalist Simone Biles pulled herself from the Olympic competition because she knew that she wasn't mentally in a good place. She was criticized, belittled, and told to suck it up. I was in awe of how she handled it. She revealed to the world the stigma around mental health that has been present for far too long.

She also illustrated something that I learned along my own journey: when I embraced who I truly was and stopped letting my mental health define me, it changed me as a pastor, a husband, and a father. To truly change your life, you have to start by looking inward and taking inventory of yourself.

The first step toward change is *mindfulness*, something I will talk about in-depth in these pages. Every journey begins with a first step. I hope that in sharing my healing journey, it will help someone take their first step.

There are two things that I want to be clear about before we begin. The first is that I have tried to weave the theme of *caring* through the pages of this book. There was one word that kept coming up time and time again: care. In terms of mental health, we don't take the time to care for ourselves. We go to great lengths for our physical health, but we don't care for our mental health. In terms of others, we seem to be living in a culture that doesn't care. We don't care what our neighbors may be going through and we don't care about how our words and actions might affect others.

The second thing I want to be clear about is that I am not pointing fingers at anyone in this book. I hold no grudges; I have forgiven. Forgiveness is part of the healing process and it's not so much about the other person as it is about *us*. Forgiveness is about *our* release. I had plenty of faults for which I had to forgive *myself*.

Again, this is my story. It's a story about my flaws and my fallibility. It's a story about my journey and what I learned along the way. It's a story about my lowest of lows, my highest of highs, and the people who helped me along the way. But it's just as much my spouse's story, my children's story, and my friends' story as it is mine. *When you're broken on the ground, you will be found.* They found me and were there for me. The person suffering from mental health is never the *only* one who suffers. Everyone who loves that person is into that world and it's just as hard on them.

This is *also* a story for others who struggle with mental health issues. As I've told my story, others have opened up about their own struggles and I've been forced to ask myself: How many more? How many others – pastors or not – are struggling in the silence, afraid to say anything? If this book can help just one person, one couple, one family, then it will have all been worth it.

I hope that telling my story will help others and bring awareness to everyone else. If you are struggling right now, I urge you to reach out and ask for help. There is no shame in that. You can embrace it; you don't have to let it define you.

So let the sun come streaming in, you'll reach up and you *will* rise again.

Part One

Have You Ever Felt Like Nobody Was There?

When the Dark Comes Crashing Through

I packed a bag and walked out of the house. As I closed the door behind me, I heard one of my kids ask, "Is daddy going to come back?" At that point, I honestly didn't know. I never expected *any* of this. The thought came creeping in that perhaps this was it, my marriage was over. *What have I done? Will our relationship end over something as insignificant as a damned pot lid?* For the first time in my life, I wondered if I even wanted to go on.

The whole thing began on New Year's Day, just after we returned from a camping trip with some of our friends. We had planned a relaxing few days away—drinking around the campfire, playing dominos, and letting the kids ride their bikes all over Yogi Bear Campgrounds. But it was cold, very cold, and not relaxing *at all*.

I don't remember exactly what went wrong at the campsite but work had been abnormally stressful as well. After all, as a pastor, you can never *truly* get away. You can try, but for some reason, all the problems seem to find you. The best escape I've managed thus far was a cruise—people can't reach you if you're in the middle of the ocean with no cell service.

Now to say things were tense around the church at that time would be an understatement. It wasn't anything that was going on with the congregation as a whole but rather struggles with leadership. I hadn't been getting along very well with a key lay leader at the church. I felt like I couldn't do anything right in this person's eyes.

I also felt that doubt was being cast upon my leadership. I really struggle when my integrity is called into question, especially since that was *the* issue that resulted in my resignation from my previous congregation. This particular lay leader wanted a record of every single moment of my ministry. I was to keep a log of my hours and activities, every minute of the day.

The church council had also asked this of other staff as well—as if we needed to justify our salaries. I honestly believe money was at the root of it all, even though they wouldn't admit it. I hate feeling mistrusted. At the time, we had been having major disagreements on this issue and several other issues around the congregation.

During Christmastime, a member yelled at me in the church lobby in front of a crowd of other worshippers simply because the service hadn't been "traditional" and none of the worship assistants wore robes. Yes, you read that correctly. All I wanted was to preside over the Christmas Eve service and then spend the holidays with my family so I buried it all. I kept it deep down inside and pretended like everything was all right.

I'm not here to point fingers. I truly believe that this lay leader's actions, based on the financial audit he was conducting, came from an honest desire to do what was best for the congregation. I truly believe now that he wasn't intentionally out to get me. But I also believe that he had no idea how much stress and anxiety I was experiencing due to his extensive probing and apparent mistrust.

Although, admittedly, I was also at fault. When it comes to mental health, there are two negative ways in which we deal with it: we bury it or we flee from it. I ended up doing both. I buried it at first.

When we bury it, we can never be truly present. In the spiritual world, this is called *mindfulness*. It requires attention and awareness, which, by the way, are universal human qualities. In his book *Wherever You Go, There You Are*, author Jon Kabat-Zinn writes, "Mindfulness means paying attention in a particular way: on purpose, in the present moment, and nonjudgmentally." It helps us come to a greater acceptance of our present reality. I may have physically been there that Christmas, and at the campground, but I really wasn't. I was doing a disservice to my friends, to my family, and to myself.

After returning home from that long camping trip, all I wanted to do was open a beer and watch my Texas Longhorns on their New Year's Day bowl against Georgia. Of course, we had to unpack the truck first and cook dinner. Things were hectic.

I hurriedly tried to unload the dishwasher so we could make room for the dinner dishes when I dropped a glass lid from our new set of pots and pans onto the floor. It shattered everywhere. At that moment, I shattered as well. All the pent-up anger, frustration, anxiety, and hopelessness of the past few months came crashing down along with it.

Now maybe you're saying to yourself, *It's just a lid, Brad. Come on.* Yes, it was just a lid, and it may seem insignificant, but that was the straw that broke the camel's back. It may have been small on its own, but when you add it up with all the other pieces, it was the size of a mountain. That lid was my final straw.

I yelled at the top of my lungs, "Fuuuuuuck! Son of a bitch! That was a brand-new *fucking* pot and pan set!" Yes, I said those things—in front of my wife and kids. I wasn't happy about my words at the time and I'm still not proud of them to this day. My wife glared at me and said, "What the hell is wrong with you? That's it. Get out. Just get out of here."

She meant for me to get out of the kitchen but I took it as an order to leave the house entirely. No doubt we had been struggling long before this. I brought home too much anxiety and stress from work and I was not letting my wife in on my struggle. I was taking it out on her and the kids.

My kids started becoming afraid of me. They wouldn't talk to me or tell me things because they thought I might lose my temper and yell at them. The worst feeling a father can have is the feeling that his children are afraid of him. That's exactly where I was.

I left the house, got in my truck, and went down to the local World of Beer restaurant nearby. I sat down and started drinking. As the football game played on the TV above the bar, it took everything in me not to cry into my beer.

I was gone for quite a while. I can't remember how long I was at the bar, but it had to have been at least three or four hours because I remember watching the game until the end. My wife had tried to call me, but I just let it go to voicemail. I knew I couldn't drink all night and that alcohol wouldn't solve any of my issues, so, at some point, I stopped and began drinking water to ensure that I was all right to drive.

But drive where? Would I go stay at a friend's house? Would I go back home? Finally, I picked up the phone and listened to my wife's voicemail. It absolutely wrecked me. I still have it saved on my phone as a sobering reminder of where I was and where I *never* want to be again.

By the time I left the bar, it was late enough that perhaps I could go back home and they would all be asleep. I could sneak in, pass out on the couch, and deal with it all in the morning. I decided to drive home, not knowing what I would find when I got there.

Many of you may be familiar with the famous story of the prodigal son.[2] In the Bible, Jesus tells his disciples a parable about a young man who took his portion of his father's estate and squandered it all. He fell so low that he ate the food from a pigsty. He finally swallows his pride and decides to return home.

Despite his shame and humiliation, he knew his only choice was to go back and beg for forgiveness. After all, he had shattered his father's heart. In that story, there is a line that says this: "and when we came to himself …" Even in his suffering, he found himself again.

---

[2] Holy Bible, Luke 15:11-32

After listening to my wife's voicemail, I, too, was at the lowest of my lows. I, too, had shattered my wife's heart. But in the parable, before the young man could offer even a word of apology, his father came running out to him, lovingly embraced him, and welcomed him back into the family. He had been waiting for him. Watching. Hoping.

I walked into the house that night and immediately went into the media room where I curled up into a fetal position on the couch and began crying my eyes out. My wife was still awake, waiting and hoping that I would come home.

Before I could offer even a word of apology, she hurried into the room, wrapped her arms around me, and silently held me for what felt like hours. I was scared as hell—terrified. There's a line in the film *The Shawshank Redemption* where the character Red, played by Morgan Freeman, says, "It's hell to live in fear. All I want is to be in a place where I ain't afraid anymore." Well, that was me.

Through my tears, I told her, "I don't want to be like this anymore. I'm sorry for hurting you." As my wife held me, she simply responded, "I'm here. We will get you help." I didn't even get out how sorry I was; the embrace *was* forgiveness. It was care and grace that far outweighed *anything* I deserved.

Things were going to have to change. I had to change. I had to be *better*, both for my family and for myself. I always thought that a person's life had to reach rock bottom for something like this to happen, but it doesn't. I had a great life. I had a beautiful home that we had recently moved into, a supportive family, a loving wife, and two amazing kids.

I *still* have a great life. Perhaps that's what made it harder to accept. Jay Shetty once wrote, "Ignoring mental health will only make you weaker."[3] I had been ignoring it for far too long and it had weakened me in every way possible.

---

[3] Shetty, Jay. *6 Ways to Protect Your Mental Health on the Job*. www. jayshetty.me, February 2022..

That night was the first episode in what would become a two-year struggle. In the days that followed, I couldn't think clearly. For one, I wasn't on any medication. I didn't know who to turn to or what to do. Remember what I said earlier about *bury or flee?* I was done dealing with the mess at the church. I was done with the church leader who I perceived was out to get me.

Every January new leaders are elected. At that particular time, leadership had recently changed over and a new person had come on board but it didn't matter. It was the church that had driven me to that dark place and I was just *done.*

I had to find a way out, or so I thought. I needed a way to distract myself from what was happening at the church. Just because the individual in question was no longer a member of the council, that didn't necessarily mean things were going to automatically get better. He had an influence on the congregation. Policies were still in place.

So I went into flight mode. *What can I do that will take me out of this situation and still help me provide for my family?* As a matter of fact, I had a real estate license and a friend who could help me flip houses. He could purchase them, through me, and then sell them, through me. I could simply be the *transactional* part of it all. *Can I make a living off of this? Can I feed my family?* I seriously doubted it, but I wanted to see what would happen.

Well, it just so happened that when my license was activated, it became public information. The wife of the former lay leader found my name and picture on the county real estate association website. Did she come to me about it? No! She went directly to a former judiciary leader of our synod. As I mentioned in the introduction, far too often we don't take the time to care about how our actions might affect others, nor do we care what others may be going through.

I remember the phone call vividly. I wasn't expecting it, nor did I have even the slightest clue how it would go. He told me about his conversation with the former council member's wife and asked me to explain myself.

And the dam broke. I poured my heart out about the struggles I had been having over the past year, my anxiety, and my breakdown. I explained that I was having a "flight" moment and unsure about ministry. "If this is the way it is going to be, then I don't know if I want to be a part of it," I told him. His response was simple. "It seems as though one of our pastors at one of our larger congregations is seeking a second job and I think you need to resign." *Excuse me?*

I sat in my home office, staring out the window for what seemed like an eternity. Out of everything I had told him, *that* was his first response. He didn't hear the pain. He didn't hear my cry for help. All he heard was that I apparently had a second job and was shirking my duties as a pastor—which was the furthest thing from the truth. There wasn't an ounce of caring in the conversation.

I was shocked and hurt. Looking back on that phone call, I might have expected something more along the lines of, "I hear that one of our pastors is struggling mentally, so how can we help you? What can we do for you?" Instead, I was simply told to resign. It was a truly uncaring conversation. It was an act of mental violence. It was a wound to my soul—one from which I am *still* trying to heal.

All the things I had learned in seminary about pastoral care were *not* on display by my local adjudicatory. My heart was broken. The church I grew up in, the Lutheran Church, seemed to be turning its back on me. The Church has a long way to go when it comes to mental health and mental health awareness.

There are certain things I've learned in dealing with people who struggle with mental health. If you truly do care about a person, here's how a conversation with them ought to go:

- Listen without making judgments and concentrate on their needs in that moment
- Ask them what would help
- Avoid confrontation
- Ask if there is someone they'd like you to contact
- Let them know you are there for them

Too often we communicate with people from where *we* are and not from where *they* are, which was exactly what the judicatory leader had done. We know more about mental health today than we ever have. We know more of the vocabulary so we must learn to communicate with those who struggle.

The judicatory leader told me he was going to call the current head of church leadership and let him know what was going on. I asked if I could contact him first. Fortunately, he agreed. I reached out to our new leader and told him everything that was happening. I said that if I needed to, I would write that letter of resignation and have it to him as soon as possible.

His response wasn't *remotely* what I had expected. "Pastor," he said, "I will not accept any letter of resignation. We'll work this out. It isn't a big deal in my eyes. I will take care of it. You just focus on taking care of yourself—that's what matters most. And let me know how I can help."

Take care of myself.

Okay… but how?

Broken On the Ground

I'm reminded of what my friend Rozella White wrote in her book *Love Big*, that "despite our brokenness, I believe healing is possible."[4] And while it's possible, it certainly doesn't happen overnight. Over the next year and a half, I learned that lesson the hard way.

I can't tell you how many phone numbers I called trying to find a psychiatrist, but I knew it was too many when my thumbs started making involuntary dialing gestures during dinner one night. The first problem had been finding a doctor with halfway decent reviews and the second had been finding one that would take my insurance. As a pastor and an employee of the ELCA, I am covered by the insurance for the church as a whole.

Of course, I thought that was all well and good. So, I called our care coordinators—people appointed by the church to help us navigate the insurance world—and I was sent a list of psychiatrists who were "in-network." It was eight pages long.

One by one, I began to search each name on Google to check their distance from me. If they were too far away, I simply marked them off. Then I ranked the rest by ones and twos—ones being closer and twos a distance I was willing to drive. It was then that I sat down and began making calls.

The whole process was frustrating, to say the least. Many psychiatrists on the list simply didn't deal with the insurance I had anymore. Some were no longer practicing and others weren't

---

[4] White, Rozella Haydée. *Love Big: The Power of Revolutionary Relationships to Heal the World*. Fortress Press, 2019, p. xxiii

actually "in-network" after all. There was one particular call that gave me a glimmer of hope.

> Office: "What insurance do you have?"
>
> Me: "BlueCross BlueShield."
>
> Office: "Is it a PPO?"
>
> Me: "Yes, ma'am. That's what it says on my card."
>
> Office: "Do you know if it is ..." [and here she tells me the name of two insurance companies]
>
> Me: "No, I have BlueCross BlueShield."
>
> Office: "Yes, I know, but they don't specifically deal in mental health. They contract that part out with either of these two companies. Do you know which one?"
>
> Me: "I have no idea."
>
> Office: "That's fine, just call your insurance provider and ask them which of the two they contract with for mental health."
>
> Me: "Okay."
>
> Office: "I'll go ahead and set an appointment for you and then you can call me back and we can begin the paperwork."
>
> Me: "Sounds good."

It seemed simple enough at first—*seemed* being the key word here. I proceeded to call back my care coordinator, sit on hold for 30 minutes, and ask which of the two insurance companies they were contracted with so that I could get *their* telephone number. It took a while because the coordinator hadn't been sure what I was asking. She put me on a brief hold to consult with a supervisor.

Once that whole rigmarole was completed, I called the psychiatrist's office again to provide the necessary information. And that's when a once-promising conversation began to go completely off the rails...

> Office: "Great! That's the one we accept. Now we can get you started. What's your ID number?"
>
> Me: "For BlueCross BlueShield?"

Office: "No, it would be the ID number for the contracted company."

Me: "Ma'am, I have no idea. I didn't even know this existed until today."

Office: "You'll need to call that insurance company and ask them for your member ID. They should be able to look you up based on your social security number."

Me: "Alright, I'll call you back."

Ugh... *okay*. So now I had to call this contracted insurance company to ask for my member ID. *Yay*. And after being on hold for *another* 45 minutes, the following conversation ensued:

Me: "Hello, so I hear my mental health coverage is contracted through you by BlueCross BlueShield. Is this correct?"

Insurance: "Yes, that is correct."

Me: "Well, I need some information in order to get an appointment."

Insurance: "Okay, let's look you up in the system. What are the last four of your social and your date of birth?"

Me: [I tell her both]

Insurance: "Okay, Brad Otto?"

Me: "Yes, that's correct."

Insurance: "Okay, great. So what is it that you're needing?"

Me: "I need my member ID."

Insurance: "Oh, that's easy. It is the same number that's on your BlueCross BlueShield insurance card."

[insert face palm emoji]

At this point, my head hit the kitchen table.

Insurance: "Now, when you call them, tell them that you have an EAP plan."

Me: "What's that?"

Insurance: "It's an Employee Assistance Program. You get six visits covered per year."

Me: "Oh, okay."

She went on to explain a few other things, but, my friends,

I was so exhausted and checked out by this point that I didn't hear a word she said. For all I knew, she could have been giving me detailed instructions on how to replace the carburetor of a 1963 Buick. Either way, once the entire spiel was over with, I proceeded to call back the doctor's office.

Me: "Okay, I have the ID number and it's the same as my BlueCross BlueShield number."

Office: "Alright, let me have that."

Me: [I give it to her] "I'm also supposed to tell you that I'm part of an EAP plan."

Office: "Oh, you are. Well, unfortunately, we don't take those types of plans. I'm sorry."

Me: "So you're telling me that after all this I'm not covered for your office?"

Office: "That's correct. You would have to pay out of pocket which is $300."

Me: "Per visit?!?"

Office: "Unfortunately, yes."

I hung up. *Drained. Dejected. Defeated.* It's no wonder why people neglect mental health in our country! Just for a minute, think about that ridiculous back-and-forth that lasted almost an entire day. Even if the place had taken my EAP plan, I was still only covered for *six* office visits all year. Once that is up, it's $300 a visit. My only hope was a Groupon!

After two more calls, I found an office that accepted my insurance plan. My first appointment was... just *okay*. The psychiatrist hadn't said much. I told him what was going on and after discussing my symptoms and my actions, he thought it might be one of two things: anxiety or ADHD.

"Have you ever been tested for ADHD?" he asked. No, I hadn't. The idea that I might have ADHD had never even crossed my mind. He wanted to try treating me for that first because he thought dealing with it might help in other areas of my life as well.

So at the psychiatrist's suggestion, I signed up for an ADHD test which ended up being the weirdest test of my life. Basically, they put this camera on you along with some other little electrodes and as you answer a bunch of boring questions, it measures how well you can keep your attention. After a few weeks, I was called in to meet with the doctor for my results. "You definitely have ADHD, Brad," he told me. *Really?* I had gone my entire life without knowing any of this. I always did well in school, I graduated in the top 10% of my class in high school, and finished college with a 3.75 GPA, so ADHD never once crossed my mind.

Can adults suddenly get ADHD? The short answer is no, they can't. Most signs tend to be evident before age 12. In other words, if you have it as an adult, then you had it as a child. Now, I don't blame my parents for this. I grew up in a day and age in which ADHD was hardly even discussed. More than likely, I was "just being a boy." The disorder can manifest in different ways at different ages; however, if the symptoms didn't present themselves during childhood, it could have been the result of something else, such as depression, anxiety, or another mood disorder.

I was prescribed Adderall and things went swimmingly for the first week or so. Then the trouble started. Heart trouble. Fortunately, I knew something was up thanks to my Apple Watch. It would alert me that my heart rate was high and, folks, it alerted me *a lot*. I couldn't keep my heart rate below 120 BPM so I called my doctor and he quickly advised me to wean my way off the drug.

Additionally, due to my family history of heart disease, he suggested that I see a cardiologist just to be sure my heart could handle taking a stimulant drug. While the symptoms *can* go away after your body gets used to it, my doctor wanted to be sure. Needless to say, I'm glad he did.

I found a cardiologist and made an appointment for a full scan of my heart. A few weeks later, I went back in for a stress test only to discover that I *also* had high blood pressure. Before the exam even began my blood pressure read 160/98 which is around where it should be toward the *height* of the stress test. Eventually, my cardiologist put me on blood pressure medicine and told me that, based on my family history and my response to such a stimulant, I shouldn't be on Adderall any longer.

As an alternative, my psychiatrist chose to put me on a non-stimulant drug called Strattera for my ADHD. For a while, all seemed to be well. Unfortunately, about eight months into taking the medication I began noticing changes in my body—I seem to be extremely sensitive to drug side effects.

I experienced a huge decrease in my appetite and was hardly eating anything. I just didn't feel like it. I also had huge mood swings. I would be cheerful one minute and moody the next. Then came the insomnia. It wasn't bad at first, but I wasn't getting a healthy amount of sleep. Little did I know that this would begin a long spiral down to the depths of a mental health hole into which I was about to sink.

It was now the end of January 2021 and I had been on this mental health journey for a year. I had been through the huge meltdown, been diagnosed with ADHD, had reactions to both stimulant *and* non-stimulant medications, and began experiencing mood swings and insomnia.

Then February rolled around and Texas was hit by the mother of all snowstorms. We hadn't seen ice and snow like that in literally *decades*. No one was prepared for it, especially the people in charge of the power grid. Seriously, mention the power grid to any Texan and you'll probably see signs of PTSD. It was *horrible*. Hundreds died because of the widespread power loss due to sub-zero temperatures.

During our second night of freezing without power, the kids were sleeping together in one room, curled up under a pile of blankets. My wife and I were in another room huddled close to one another, desperately hoping our body heat would keep us warm. I never thought it could get *that* cold in our house. I wore pajama pants, sweatpants, three layers of shirts, the warmest socks I could find, and was wrapped in at least three blankets. You may laugh, but that's how cold it was. Exhausted, anxious, and unable to sleep, I got up and wandered into the media room, where I eventually dozed off on the couch.

But then something jolted me awake.

I couldn't breathe. I was shaking—not because of the cold—and there was an overwhelming tightness in my chest. Scared to death, I hurried into the other room to wake my wife.

"Babe, something's wrong," I said.

"What is it?"

"I'm shaking. I can't stop shaking and I can't breathe!"

"Okay, let's go sit down," she replied as she helped me into the media room once again. "What else are you feeling?"

I told her I couldn't breathe and that my chest felt tight. Fearing a heart attack, she decided to call 911. My father had a heart attack at age 42, the same age I was then. It's crazy to think about, but that's exactly what was running through my mind. I was reminded of a line from *The Lords of the Rings*, "and so it begins..."

Thankfully, the amazing men and women from the Cypress Fairbanks Fire Department arrived within 20 minutes... *in the ice and snow.* When they checked my vitals, my heart rate and blood pressure were through the roof. I told them I was experiencing tightness in my chest and the next thing I knew I was being loaded into the back of an ambulance.

After that, the details are a bit fuzzy, but I remember a slow and bumpy ride to the hospital due to the road conditions, an IV being inserted into my arm, an EMS worker telling me he was going to give me something or other through that IV, and then a nitro patch being placed on my chest, just in case. By the time we reached the hospital, my vitals were beginning to come down, but it was still an all-night affair.

I sat in a chair in the waiting room because all the beds were full due to COVID-19. They took me back and forth for tests, gave me some more medication through the IV, and also gave me some Tylenol for the headache I received from the nitro patch. Long story short, it turned out to be a full-blown panic attack. What I didn't know at the time was that panic attacks can mirror heart attacks in many ways. According to Johns Hopkins, both a panic attack *and* a heart attack can cause feelings of extreme agitation and terror, dizziness, chest pain, stomach discomfort, shortness of breath, and rapid heart rate.

Needless to say, there was *zero* sleep that night. My wife put the kids in the car and picked me up after carefully navigating the icy conditions. She used alternate routes to avoid bridges and overpasses, so when I say my wife has put her life on the line for me, I mean it!

All in all, 2021 would end up being the year of insomnia and panic attacks for me. I made several trips to the emergency room that year—at *least* three, as I recall—one of them while on vacation at the beach. I had no idea what was happening. Each time I received morphine and some anti-nausea medication, they'd run some tests, and then send me on my way. Soon I began to associate sleep with panic attacks, apparently developing some form of PTSD after the event in February.

I signed up finally for BetterHelp.com and sought out a therapist to help talk me through it all. The first therapist wasn't much help. I felt like he wasn't listening to me and he kept giving me the same advice over and over again so I decided to try another one. Unfortunately, the second therapist wasn't much of an improvement and the service was costing me $300 a month. That was a lot for our family. Still, things *had* to get better, right? Little did I know that the worst was yet to come.

Forgotten in the
Middle of Nowhere

I grew up on a rural farm in Fayette County, Texas, out in the hill country between La Grange and Schulenburg. It was a German farm where my grandparents—on my mother's side of the family—actually still spoke German. We moved back there from Austin in the early '80s. Shortly thereafter, my grandfather died early from cancer.

I can't remember much about him, just that he was a farmer with a huge personality whom everyone loved. One thing I do remember is sitting on his lap a time or two while he drove the tractor. In those few precious moments, I was as happy as I'd ever been. Perhaps that's why those are some of the few memories that I retained. The rest I've had to hear in stories.

But in all of those stories, I never heard what my mom finally told me before I left for the hospital: my grandfather had a mental health episode when he was about the same age as me. He went off to get help and came back a better man because of it. Imagine my surprise when I found out. *Why the hell am I just hearing about it now?* Well, because you didn't talk about those things. You *did* talk about the fond memories (and of course, you could talk about cancer), but *never* mental health. It seemed as though my hidden family history was about to make a grand entrance into the script of my life.

By the end of August 2021, my insomnia had gone from bad to worse. It appeared that I was beginning to develop sleep anxiety—a feeling of intense stress or fear about going to sleep.

Anxiety is the most common mental health disorder in the United States, affecting more than 40 million adults. Research suggests that most people with mental health disorders also have some form of sleep disruption.

I also believe that I had some sort of *somniphobia* stemming from my panic attack in the middle of the night back in February. Somniphobia is when you believe (even subconsciously) that something terrible will happen while you are asleep. It often develops as a form of PTSD. I'd call a severe panic attack in the middle of a February snowstorm pretty traumatic. Needless to say, sleep and psychiatric disorders, especially anxiety, often go hand in hand.

The last week of August heading into Labor Day weekend had been the worst. In those seven days, I got a total of six hours of sleep. Yes, for the *entire* week. It didn't matter what I did or what medications I took, I simply could not go to sleep. I would get to the point of falling asleep and then have little jerks that would jolt me awake. Later, I found out that these were called *hypnic jerks*, for which I eventually received treatment.

Those were some of the longest and loneliest nights I have ever experienced. I was already anxious and adding an additional layer of anxiety about whether or not I would fall asleep certainly did not help. Honestly, I don't know how I functioned at all during the days, but I do know that whenever the sun set, my anxiety kicked into overdrive and the darkness took over.

It was *horrible* at night. *Crippling. Debilitating.* I would lay there for hours on end, watching the clock as endless seconds slowly ticked by. Voices whispered in my head telling me I should get to sleep, but as soon as I began to doze off, my body would jerk awake.

I tried everything I could think of—Benadryl, Tylenol PM, sometimes both at the same time. I even took CBD oil to help me relax, but nothing worked. After eventually growing tired of reading, I would set up my iPad and turn on an old episode of

Fraiser, one of my favorite sitcoms. I loved the show, but I had seen it so many times that I figured I could zone out, turn off my brain, and eventually drift off to sleep. I also laughed at the idea that I had developed a relationship with Dr. Fraiser Crane—a psychologist, ironically enough—and wanted to call in to see if he had any advice. So, Kelsey Grammer, if you're reading this, thank you for listening.

After an excruciatingly long week, I had to preside over a funeral on the Saturday of Labor Day weekend. On the way, I stopped at a gas station and got a Red Bull. I *desperately* needed that extra energy to get through the day. No one knew what was going on behind the scenes. I didn't want them to. In fact, I needed to make *sure* they didn't know. I remember talking to our deacon before the funeral began and telling her I had been having issues sleeping. "Perhaps after the service, you can go home and take a good nap," she suggested. *Yes, perhaps.*

I finished the funeral, grabbed a quick bite to eat in the fellowship hall, and then headed home. On the way, I called to check in with my wife. She and the kids were out and about with my parents and my son had a belt ceremony for his Tae Kwon Do class later. Sensing an opportunity to get some much-needed rest, I took off my dress clothes as soon as I got home and collapsed on the bed. But once again, just as I was beginning to fall asleep, those perky hypnic jerks snapped me awake.

So yeah... to say that I was frustrated would be the understatement of the century.

I tried for another 15 minutes or so but jerk after jerk would wake me just as I was dozing off. *Every. Single. Time.* I couldn't even sleep during the damn day! I knew I needed help. Like the lyrics to that Matchbox 20 song said, I was headed for a breakdown and it was coming fast. But I had no idea where to start.

My parents arrived back at the house before my wife with the kids in tow. Thankfully, the kids went straight to their bedrooms.

As for me? I was a complete mess. I had been sitting at the kitchen table searching online for some sort of help, be it psychiatric or pharmaceutical or *whatever*. Unfortunately, I couldn't find any options that allowed me to speak to someone immediately. The earliest available appointment was the following Tuesday and I absolutely could not go on any longer without sleep.

My head was on the table and I was crying and muttering gibberish. After noticing the state I was in, my parents asked what was wrong. Through the tears, slobber, and mess, the floodgates opened and I told them everything. By the time I'd finished explaining, my wife had arrived home. After my parents told her how they'd found me, she became determined to get me help.

My parents distracted the kids and Stacie took me to her office in the front bedroom, away from little eyes and ears. They didn't need to see me in this state; they didn't need to have this on their plates. Yes, I would tell the kids at *some* point, but now was not the time. They would just get scared and worry, which would only add to my already debilitating anxiety. Although I didn't know it when we first walked into her office, my wife had already found a mental health hospital that would admit me that day. All I had to do was agree to be checked in voluntarily within the next two hours.

A mental hospital? I had seen them on TV but I didn't know what to expect. Would it be a cushy-looking place like the ones celebrities check themselves into? Would it be like the rehab facility where Sandra Bullock stayed in *28 Days*? Or would it be one of those creepy places filled with straight jackets and padded rooms like you see in horror films? Arkham Asylum from the Batman comics was the only thing I had in my mind.

I remember sitting on the floor with my neighbor, who is a dear friend, along with Stacie and my parents, curled up in a ball crying about how terrified I was to go. That's when my mom told me about my grandfather.

My mother doesn't remember much, since she was only a

young girl at the time, but she knew *something* was going on. My grandparents were farmers and existed at the mercy of Mother Nature. As such, they were financially strapped and had loans on tractors and combines, on top of vet bills for cattle and a million other expenses. My grandmother never let on much, of course. *You simply didn't talk about those things.* She just told my mom that my grandfather wasn't doing well, so they went to stay at my great-grandparents' house.

Later she found out that my grandfather was scared and had threatened to hurt himself. Fortunately, my great-grandfather was able to talk him down and keep him calm They watched over him until the next day when he went into town to see his general practitioner who gave him some medication—there weren't any psychiatrists or mental hospitals in a small town in rural Texas and you *certainly* kept stuff like this quiet so no one would know.

After agonizing over it for a while, I finally decided, *screw it, I need to go.* Both for my family and myself. I packed a bag with what I was allowed to bring: shoes with no laces, two t-shirts, pants and shorts with no tie strings, books to read, and toiletries. That was it. I would be completely cut off. No phone, no iPad, no electronics at all. And *that* is what scared me the most. No, not the electronics, but the fact that I would be cut off from the ones I loved. The ones who kept me going; the ones I lived for.

I came close to having another panic attack just sitting in the parking lot of the hospital. For what seemed like an eternity, I couldn't even find the strength to open the door. However, after a few deep breaths and a pep talk by my wife, I finally worked up the courage to leave the car and step inside.

An intake nurse asked me a bunch of preliminary questions. I'm sure they were about my medical history, the drugs that I was taking, my symptoms... but, to tell you the truth, I don't remember a single one of them. I only remember staring down at the floor in a daze, as if lost in a dream.

After the nurse finished checking me in, they confiscated my bag so they could root through my personal items to check for contraband. And while that was humiliating enough, it paled in comparison to what happened next. A large, intimidating man lead me into a nearby bathroom and asked me to strip naked. He then checked every crevice I had—*every crevice*. In that moment, it wasn't just my clothing that had been stripped away, but every last shred of my dignity.

Who am I? Has it really all come to this? As I stood there, enduring a full-body cavity search with my nakedness and frailty both fully exposed, it felt more like punishment than treatment. There's a line from the musical *Hamilton* that reminded me this could happen to anyone: "Life doesn't discriminate between the sinners and the saints."

Once the examination was over and I had re-dressed, it was time to say goodbye to my wife. For the longest time, we just held each other, crying. She promised that I'd get better and I apologized profusely for putting her in this situation. When it comes to those of us who suffer from mental health issues, as Shakespeare famously wrote, "Aye, there's the rub." We feel like we've broken the law or committed some heinous crime, but that's simply not the case.

It's an *illness*. It's something you can't help. It's a part of who you are. So if you're reading this and you're struggling with mental health, or if someone close to you is struggling, please hear me when I say: *You are a beloved child of God. They are beloved children of God.* People who struggle with mental health aren't broken. They're not rejects, outcasts, or freaks.

When I finally let go of my wife and the hospital door slammed behind me, I felt utterly and completely lost. I felt like I had failed as a husband, as a father, and as a pastor. Hell, I felt like I had failed as a human being. And with the slamming of that heavy wooden door, the last lingering glimmer of hope within me seemed to die.

I didn't know it then but, as Andy Dufrain says in *The*

Shawshank Redemption, "Hope is a good thing... a good thing that never dies." Somehow, I had to hold on to that. But instead, all I could think about was the sign above the entrance to Hell in Dante's *Divine Comedy*: "Abandon all hope, ye who enter here."

The nurses showed me to my room and I met my roommate. He didn't talk—at *all*. He either sat there staring at the wall, laid on his bed like a mummy with the covers pulled up to his neck, or paced. I would normally be able to ignore the pacing, but he had squeaky shoes. Sometimes I can still hear them inside my head when everything else is quiet. At one point, I wanted to rip them off of his feet and say, "Dude, if you're gonna pace, at least pace in your socks!"

Later, they showed me around. The common room was much as I expected it to be. There were several couches around the perimeter, a table and chairs for board games, a piano in the corner, and a TV on the wall complete with a DVD collection. When I walked into the common room, I remember all the heads turning to stare at me.

A couple of guys in the corner started whispering to one another and laughing and I began to worry that I might get shanked. I heard one of the women say, "Fuck! Just what we need, another one." *Well, great to meet you, too!* One guy just stared at me with this evil look and shit-eating grin—a rather creepy, disturbing expression that remained plastered across his face my entire stay.

Not exactly the warmest welcome.

And then there was Johnny. *Oh, Johnny.* He fidgeted the entire time. He also mumbled when he talked so I couldn't understand a word he said. I'd politely nod and smile. Johnny always wanted a smoke break. The orderly would yell back, "You get a damn smoke break when it's time to get a smoke break!" and then the two of them would fight for a few minutes until he was ordered to go back to his room. Unfortunately, whenever Johnny was in his room, he liked to sing (or more accurately shout) '80s rock songs at the top of his lungs.

Sally was one of the friendlier patients. She shook my hand and had a huge smile on her face. Her skin was burned all over—it looked like scales. I eventually learned that she was a self-harmer who liked to burn herself and that served as a vivid reminder that when you think your situation is bad, remember, there might be others who have it *far* worse.

Of course, shortly afterward, a young man in his early twenties sat down next to me, introduced himself, and said, "Be careful with Sally. She just wants to get into every guy's pants. You're new, so she's probably going to try extra hard for you." *What the hell is happening? Am I supposed to get help in here?*

Tom, that helpful young man, and I became very close during my short hospital stay.

I spent the rest of the day reading and watching movies in the common room. Some of the girls were putting together a puzzle, Johnny was begging for a smoke break, and those two men were still in their corner looking around and laughing ominously at everyone. It was unsettling, to say the least. Fortunately, movies have a way of transporting us to a different world and allowing us to get lost in time and space. I desperately needed that—as a stranger in a *very* strange land—and it was probably the only thing that got me through that first day.

Eventually, I went to my room to read and try and take my mind off things. I was only there for about 15 minutes before nurse Rachel came in and said, "I have some good news. I talked to your doctor and we are going to be giving you three types of medication. You'll be taking 30mg of Buspar three times daily, 15mg of Atarax three times daily, and 160mg of Doxepin at night.

"The Buspar is to prevent anxiety attacks, the Atarax is to help whenever you *do* feel anxious—although hopefully, we'll be able to slowly cut back over time—and the Doxepin is to help you sleep." *Wow, that's a lot of medication.*

I could see where this was going: drug me up so that when it came to getting out, I would be so far out of it that I wouldn't be able to think straight. Of course, what else was I going to do? I needed to sleep so I took my first dose of all three.

Lights-out wasn't for another hour or so, but within 30 minutes, I was asleep. For the first time in over a week, my mind was finally at rest.

Maybe There's a
Reason to Believe

It is not easy
Healing yourself
Building new habits
Observing reality without permission or delusion
This work takes effort
But if you persist
The fruits of your labor will
Have an immensely positive
Impact on your life [5]

I slept for twelve hours. *Twelve. Hours.*

I missed breakfast, but I didn't care. Not one little bit. Rachel, my nurse, finally woke me to give me my morning medication. I needed to eat something with it so, even though she wasn't supposed to, she brought me some graham crackers and apple juice.

"How do you feel?" she asked.

"Like a new man," I answered.

"I'm so glad. You look like a new man!"

"Rachel, can I ask you something?"

"Sure, what is it?"

"I want to go home. I don't think this is the place for me—I'm

---

[5] Pueblo, Yung. *Clarity & Connection*. Andrews McMeel Publishing, 2021, p. 5

just being honest—but I'm scared of having to start all over. The thought of staying in here a long time and having to go through the court system terrifies me."

"I understand," she replied, "and you know what? I agree with you. I don't think you belong here, either. I think this is where you needed to be at this particular time because it was your only option. I tell you what, let me talk to your doctor and see what I can do. I'll still need you to fill out the form asking to be released, but I will talk to him personally about your situation."

"Thank you, Rachel, I really appreciate it."

"No problem," she said, patting me on my leg. "It might take me a while, but hang in there, I'll get you an answer soon."

"Thanks, I will."

I decided to head back to the common room for a bit. I was hoping there'd be a good movie on and I could lose myself for a little while. I took my journal with me but never actually got an opportunity to write in it. I'd walked right into the middle of a yoga session. They invited me to join, but I politely declined. Sorry, yoga fans. It's just not my thing. Instead, I took a seat over by Tom who happened to be scribbling away in his own journal.

"Hey, Tom!"

"Hey, Brad!"

"You alright?" I asked.

"Yeah, I'm doing good. Hey, I heard you were going to try and get out of here. Is that right?"

Damn, word travels fast in this place.

"Yes, but it's not a guarantee. We'll see how it goes."

"I'm thinking about signing the form as well," he responded.

"Oh really?"

"Yeh, I think I'm ready to get out. Well… *this* time."

"This time? What do you mean?"

"Oh, I've been in here a few times already. I'll be doing fine and then I'll just fall down again. When that happens, I just come back here and check myself in."

"But when you go back out, you don't get help? You don't get to stay on your meds?"

"Yeah, no meds. That's usually how it happens when you leave on your own. I try to make it for as long as I can. Then, when I'm not doing well again, I come back here."

"You don't see anyone on the outside?" I asked.

"Are you kidding? It's too damn expensive. I don't have insurance either. I'm 22 and I can barely hold down a job because of my mental issues. So I come here, get the meds I need, stay until I feel better, and then go back out into the real world until I don't."

I couldn't believe what I was hearing. It reminded me of an episode of *The Big Bang Theory* where Leonard calls a therapist looking for couples counseling for him and Penny: "Hi. I'm calling about your marriage counseling services and was curious what your rate is. Really? Um, okay. Is there any kind of discount for length of marriage? 'Cause, we're just talking hours here." Later on, he even asked about a Groupon code.[6]

Tom was a good kid—a good kid who needed continual help. It's a shame when someone can't afford to get the help that they need and their only hope is to check in to a state-run hospital for short periods, only to be released alone and unsupported back into the world. That's not getting help, that's medicating someone to see how long they can last. It's a Band-Aid response. The thing about Band-Aids is that they don't heal; they just cover up the wound to prevent further damage.

After a couple of hours, I was given another round of medication and took a nap. I was awakened once again by my nurse, Rachel.

"Hey Brad, you awake?"

"Yeah, I'm awake now. Just dozing a little."

---

[6] "The Separation Oscillation." *The Big Bang Theory*, created by Chuck Lorre and Bill Prady, season 9, episode 2, Chuck Lorre Productions and Warner Bros. Television, 2015.

"Oh, I'm sorry. I know how much you need it. But hey, I have good news! The doctor wants to talk to you and I think he might release you *with* outpatient treatment."

"Really? Are you kidding? That means I could go home *and* stay on medication?"

"Yes! Believe me, it hardly ever happens."

Rachel was a saint. Even if it didn't work, knowing I had someone in that place who was looking out for me boosted my morality. She truly cared.

It was late afternoon and I had passed the 24-hour mark. I went into the "telephone room" with Rachel where they let the patients make occasional phone calls. Since it was a Sunday, the doctor was working remotely and we talked via video chat over an iPad.

Sunday... *Wow.* I was supposed to have been at church that morning. I was supposed to have given the message and presided over communion. Once again, that feeling of failure washed over me. I felt as if I had left my ministry team in the lurch. They already did so much and I was piling on even more.

Come on, stay focused.

I sat down in front of the iPad they'd provided, ready to meet with the psychiatrist. Lo and behold, Santa Claus was staring back at me. *No really.* His hair was completely white and he had a long white beard. He was even wearing a red shirt. The background behind him was a beach scene with palm trees swaying in the wind. *So, this is what Santa does in the offseason. Not a bad gig.*

Okay, Brad, try not to laugh or they may keep you here.

He was very kind. He told me that they hardly ever do this, but he was going to release me *with* my medications as long as I agreed to seek outpatient therapy. They would provide me with the name of a psychiatrist to go see and then I could continue my treatment with that doctor. After I agreed, he went over each of the medications with me again—how many times a day, the dosage, and what each of them did. They would call these medications into whatever pharmacy I provided for Rachel.

The two of them talked back and forth about my discharge and then he wished me well. Coincidently enough, he *also* said he didn't think this was the place for me but I needed it to begin the process of becoming whole again. That's when I broke down crying.

Rachel moved over to my side of the table, hugged me, and we just sat like that for a while. I owed so much to her. She was my angel in disguise. She took the time to listen to me and to meet me where I was. She took the time to *care*.

"You want to call your wife and tell her the good news?" she asked.

Yes. Yes, I did. A full 27 hours after I'd walked through those doors, I was calling Stacie to let her know I was coming home.

Due to all the discharge paperwork, it would be a few more hours before she could pick me up. I decided to go back to the common room. Tom was over on the couch writing in his journal as usual. I sat down next to him.

"Well? What happened?" he asked.

"I'm going home. *And...* I'm going home with medication," I replied.

"Are you kidding? That *never* happens!"

"I know! I got lucky I guess."

Deep down I knew it wasn't luck. I knew God was watching over me. God sent Rachel to me for a reason. And, even though being there had been a bit unsettling, my short stay in that mental health hospital had *not* been all for nothing.

While I sat waiting for Stacie to arrive, I remembered the phone conversation I'd had with her the night before. We talked about how everything was going and she asked if I'd received any medication yet. I told her no but that I probably would shortly.

"I don't think I can heal in this place," I told her. "I don't belong here."

"I'm sorry, babe, but I didn't know where else to get you help."

"I want to try and see if I can get out. There has to be another way."

"Okay, I'm fine with that, but we'll need a plan for when you come home."

"I know..."

"Just see how tonight goes and then call me again tomorrow."

"Okay, I will. I think I have phone time again late morning or around noon."

"Sounds good. I'll talk to you then. I love you."

"I love you, too," I whimpered, choking back tears.

I had been wrong about not being able to heal. Instead, I learned that healing can come in the strangest of places. (Although my time in the hospital was just the beginning.) The first step was self-awareness. It always is. The poet Yung Pueblo wrote, "By taking a deeper look inward we may gain the courage to evolve—into greater mental clarity, into greater happiness, into greater patience, into greater honesty, into greater love."[7]

Self-awareness is an essential first step to any change. When I coach my clients, we always begin with self-awareness. It's about examining who we are and being in touch with ourselves. As the famous maxim by Socrates says, *nosce te ipsum*. Know thyself. Not only is self-awareness a necessary first step to change, but now I also believe it to be a necessary first step in *healing*. It's essential to stop us from causing harm to ourselves and others.

Later in this process, I learned that self-awareness is *also* about taking time to understand what society has placed in our minds, even subconsciously. At that point in my life, society had been telling me that I was a failure; that there was something wrong with me; that my mental health defined me. Those fears and insecurities were *toxic*. Moreover, they were flat-out wrong. The truth about myself eventually set me free.

---

[7] Pueblo, p. 14

I also learned that healing takes *time*. As a person without a whole lot of patience, that was pretty difficult for me. I thought my discharge would be the beginning of the end of this entire mess. I was dead wrong.

I had a long road ahead of me, but, oddly enough, I took the first steps toward healing during the 30 hours I spent in that hospital.

Reaching Up

I noticed on my Apple Watch that my heart rate had been slowly increasing little by little each week. *Here we go again.* I'm telling you, if there are negative side effects to medications, I'm *going* to have them. Period.

My heart rate hovered around the 100-bpm mark just sitting on the couch watching television. I had already been diagnosed with high blood pressure so I strapped my blood pressure cuff onto my arm and took the reading. I did a double take. My blood pressure read 150/91 with a heart rate of 120 bpm. Already on blood pressure medicine, my systolic usually hovered in the 115 to 120 range with the diastolic in the upper 70s to low 80s.

Hoping that maybe it was just one bad day, I tracked my blood pressure for a week. I was dismayed to discover that it stayed abnormally high. Suddenly, my sleep wasn't all that great anymore. *What is happening?* I felt like I was moving backward.

Leaving the hospital hadn't been the beginning of the end; it had actually been just the *beginning.* After I checked out, I kept my end of the bargain and scheduled a session the following week with the psychiatrist recommended by my doctor at the hospital.

When I reached the address on the day of my appointment, I pulled up to a dilapidated house. *Wait... this can't be right.* There was no sign or indication that this was even a practice at all. I checked my phone, verified the address, and walked inside.

The place was old. The carpet was nasty and I was abruptly greeted by a not-so-friendly pug who seemed rather territorial.

"Come on in," said the secretary seated toward the back of the house. "He just likes to bark."

Sure. I stepped past the dog and took a seat in the waiting room—which was just the living room—to fill out my paperwork.

Ugh... that smell is really getting to me.

Eventually, the doctor came out, welcomed me, and retrieved my paperwork from the office manager. He led me into his office—a room adjacent to the living room—and I was greeted by yet another pug. (This one was absolutely ancient.) It looked like it had mange, was half-blind, and could have keeled over at any moment.

The doctor took about five minutes just introducing me to the dog and then finally sat down behind his desk. For the next 45 minutes, he typed my information into his laptop—one letter at a time with his index fingers. He never looked up. He asked me two questions: What happened? Were the meds working? And that was it. He told me to stay on them and that we would check back in around the one-month mark. That was the extent of my appointment.

This had been my second time seeing a psychiatrist and the second time I came away feeling as though they could've cared less. Both had seemed more interested in medication than anything else. It was as if the world of psychiatry had devolved to throwing pills at people just to see what stuck. "If this medication doesn't work, we'll try another." No one bothers listening to what is going on or why the other medication may not have worked. Needless to say, I didn't come away feeling very hopeful after that initial visit.

There's a scene in *A Charlie Brown Christmas* when Charlie Brown shouts in desperation, "Isn't there anyone who can tell me what Christmas is all about?!?" That was how I felt. *Isn't there anyone who will listen to me and help me figure out what's going on?!?*

For the next month, things seemed to be going fine. I was taking my meds as I should and sleeping, for the most part. Then about four weeks later, I started noticing some shifts. While I was calm and it seemed as though my anxiety was under control, I wasn't the same. I was present but I wasn't *fully* present.

I had a birthday during that month and we went out with friends. To tell you the truth, I can't recall much about that evening. I know we went out to eat and I know we went country dancing, but beyond that... *nothing*. It's just a haze. I imagine it was all the medicine that I was on. Even my wife could tell that I wasn't myself. And *that* was when my blood pressure and heart rate both went crazy.

Panicked and shaken, I called and left a voicemail with my psychiatrist's office. About two hours later, the office manager called back and said the doctor wanted me to stop taking the medication altogether and that we could regroup when I came in to see him in about a week and a half.

I followed those instructions and stopped taking all of my medication. Cold turkey. I had no idea that I was supposed to gradually wean myself off of them. That call was on a Wednesday, by Friday I was experiencing *major* withdrawal symptoms. I felt like I had the flu. I sweat through several sets of clothes day and night. My body occasionally shook uncontrollably and I experienced moments of high anxiety and then severe depression. A few nights I just passed out next to the toilet because I kept throwing up. Needless to say, I wasn't sleeping and it seemed as though I was right back where I started, only worse.

I called the doctor the next Friday and got a recording saying that the office was closed. *At 2:00pm? Did he check his voicemails? Will he return my call? Will I have to wait the entire weekend?* My wife wisely suggested that I call the pharmacy and explain what was going on. The pharmacist immediately told me to *never* stop taking medications like the ones I was on. She couldn't believe that any decent doctor would provide such lazy advice, *especially* without giving any further instructions.

The pharmacist told me I was going through major withdrawal

and needed to course-correct fast. She was amazing. Her advice was to either push through the symptoms since I had already stopped taking my meds or to go back on them and then come down gradually (which she explained how to do). She did warn me, however, that the process would take a while and that I could still experience withdrawal symptoms.

I decided to go back on the medications and follow the pharmacist's instructions to the tee. She was absolutely right. For me to fully wean off the medications, it would be a two-week process of gradually reducing my dosage, followed by several more weeks of side effects.

I remember driving back from a pastor's meeting at Living Word Lutheran Church in Katy, Texas when out of nowhere I just started crying. I mean, I had to pull off the road because I couldn't see or concentrate on my driving. I had never been depressed before, but coming off these medications had turned me into a depressed human being. I *hated* it. I asked myself, "What is wrong with you?" over and over again. "Get a grip. Get your shit together. You have no reason to be depressed." That was my mantra. It certainly wasn't helpful.

Another incident occurred when I went to Washington DC with my wife to watch a rugby game. I'm a huge rugby fan and one of the greatest rugby teams in the world, the New Zealand All Blacks, were in town to play our national team. We flew up on a Friday in mid-October, about a month and a half after my release from the mental hospital and two weeks into coming off my psychiatric medication.

I felt like I was in a complete fog. It felt dreamlike to me. I was there, but I wasn't *there*. That evening, we took the train into DC and walked the National Mall. We saw all the sights—the Capitol Building, the Washington Monument, the World War II Monument, and the Lincoln Memorial.

By the time we made it from one end to the other, it was time for our dinner reservations near the White House at The

Hamilton. As a fan of the musical *Hamilton*, I *had* to eat at this place. But I couldn't even enjoy it. Amazing food was sitting right in front of me and I barely touched it. And then, in the middle of dinner, the waterworks started flowing.

"Why the hell am I crying?"

"It's because you're still coming off of your medication," my wife reassured me.

"I know, but I'm just tired of feeling like this. I'm tired of being depressed and walking around in a fog."

"It will get better, just give it some time."

I hated that I was ruining her first trip to DC. I hated that I was barely present. I hated that I felt completely numb to everything. I hated that I would talk but not even hear what I was saying—that I would be interacting but not really taking it all in. I would smile when I could, continuing the performance that everything was just fine and dandy, but living within that charade simply ensured that nothing was *ever* as special as I wanted it to be. I felt as though I was on the outside of my life looking in and couldn't control the narrative of what was happening. I was a stranger watching someone else's story unfold.

And that was the second time in my life that I questioned going on. I didn't see the point.

My wife was right, though. It *does* get better. Healing takes time. People heal differently and in different ways. Sometimes you think if you go one way you will find healing, only to discover that it may be down another path all together. Healing is not *forgetting* either. It is in the way you react to old triggers—how you react to the painful memories that linger in your subconscious—and the power you allow them to have over your mind.

Over the next four weeks, I slowly began to become my "normal" self again. I hope those words of care resonate with you, too. If you're reading this right now and are struggling with mental health, hear the same words my wife said to me: *It will get better.* Each hour, each day, each week, each month, it gets better.

Healing doesn't have a time limit nor does it have an ending. I believe we are *always* in a constant state of healing ourselves. I'm still healing myself and still trying to heal my family. I don't believe I'll ever fully be done with that work.

Embrace healing as a journey.

After that trip to DC, I made the conscious choice not to return to a psychiatrist and to stay off medication. I needed to find other ways of healing. Don't get me wrong, I'm not knocking psychiatry in the least—it just wasn't for *me*. Same with the medication. Many people in this world genuinely need those types of medications and find great results from them, but I wasn't one of them.

I was determined to find another way forward to deal with my sleep anxiety and my mental health. In the next few chapters, I lay out my path, but it's just that: *my* path. It's what worked for me, but that doesn't mean it will work for you. Yung Pueblo said, "each person holds a unique emotional history."[8] If you need help figuring out your own path, my website and email are located at the back of this book. Please reach out to me and I will help you however I can.

---

[8] Pueblo, p. 25

Part Two

Let the Sun Come Streaming In

Finding Myself Again

Socrates taught his disciples that an unexamined life isn't worth living. I believe that. Now the hard work begins: How do I find myself again? How do I begin the journey of healing and discovering who I am? I want to spend this chapter highlighting a few of the ways that I went about my journey of healing. This has been my path and that doesn't mean it has to be yours. Each of us finds our own ways of healing and finding our true identities. I hope that by sharing my path, it can perhaps help you to rise and start your own.

FAITH

I am a pastor so faith obviously played a role in my path to healing. However, there was a time during this journey when I was on shaky ground with God. We all reach points in our lives, even for the briefest of moments, when we find ourselves wrestling with spiritual questions. That was me. In those moments we *want* to trust God, but when we're holding on for dear life in the middle of a storm, we often doubt that we *can*.

I meet people all the time who want to believe in God's presence in the world—want to believe in His goodness and mercy—but when they look at their lives they have a hard time believing. This causes many to leave the church altogether while many others continue to come to worship week after week, trying to get a glimpse of God's presence, a pinch of peace, a morsel of mercy.

Deep down we all hope that God (however we may see God) isn't just some cosmic figure in the clouds to which we cling in hopeless naiveté. We want to know that "even though we walk through the valley of the shadow of death, we can fear no evil."[9] For a while, I was the one shouting, "Why me? Why is this happening to me? Where are you now? How is this supposed to grow my faith? I am your servant, working my ass off trying to build *your* church and *this* is what I get?" Have you shouted similar questions?

I am reminded of a passage in the Gospel of John. It's the story of Lazarus, Jesus' good friend who becomes very ill.[10] Jesus receives word that Lazarus is sick but seems to do absolutely nothing about it. He doesn't drop everything immediately and run to his bedside. I mean, this guy is supposed to be the Messiah, right? The healer? Why not go and heal his friend?

After a while, Jesus travels to Bethany to visit Lazarus' sisters, Mary and Martha, but Lazarus had already died. He had been dead for days. As he approached the sisters, they ran out to Jesus yelling, "Lord, if you would have been here my brother would not have died." A modern-day translation of that verse might say, "Lord, if you were doing your job, this would not have happened!" Have you ever shouted that out? That was me. In his book *Hope in the Dark*, Craig Groeschel wrote, "Painful trials are fertile ground for the seeds of doubt."[11] No doubt! (See what I did there?)

One thing I've learned from leading a church is that, more often than not, we'd rather talk about theology than deal with doubt and pain. We like to discuss the fluffiness of grace and love but rarely do we talk about the valley of the shadow of death. We love Easter, but we don't like to trudge through Holy Week because it's too "sad" and "depressing."

---

[9] Holy Bible, Psalm 23:4 (paraphrased)
[10] Holy Bible, John 11:1-44 NRSV
[11] Groeschel, Craig. *Hope in the Dark: Believing God Is Good When Life Is Not.* Zondervan, 2018, p. 27

The Church's avoidance of difficult issues has and continues to be a disservice to the people. We often hear preachers talk about favor and wealth and happiness for those who simply follow Jesus. Well, I was following, but nothing in my life looked like God's favor. And if it *was*, I didn't want any part of it.

I want to reiterate that asking questions about faith isn't something that should cause us shame. It doesn't reveal a lack of faith. As a matter of fact, allowing ourselves to ask those types of questions can lead us on a journey of reconnection with God. In the Bible, there is a book called Habakkuk—I know, weird name, but there are some *really* wise sayings in the writings of that minor prophet. In the second chapter he writes, "I will stand at my watch and station myself on the ramparts; I will look to see what God will say to me, and what answer I am to give..."[12]

I *love* that.

I will stand and wait for what God will say to me. *That* was one of the *first* things I had to do. I had to listen to what God was going to tell me. Our problem is that we are often too busy or too jaded to stop and listen to God's voice. Other times we don't listen for fear of what we might hear. Each of the lessons that I wrote about in this book I learned by taking time to journal, to ponder, and to listen for God's voice. As the psalmist wrote, "Be still, and know that I am God."[13] *Be still.* That's hard to do. After all, I had a church to run, sermons to write, and kids to transport to gymnastics and Tae Kwon Do practices. How could I stop and listen for God?

I recently preached through a series of sermons about not allowing our emotions to control us. Admittedly, it was a bit selfish because I sought my own healing through them. By working through topics of fear, doubt, anger, and others, I was able to address some of my own issues and struggles as well. I was forced to stop and listen to God!

---

12 Holy Bible, Habakkuk 2:1 NRSV
13 Holy Bible, Psalm 46:10 NRSV

Usually, when I get up to preach a message, I *believe* what I say. I mean... obviously, right? Why preach a message of faith if you don't have your own? Well, this was the only time that I wasn't 100% there yet. I wasn't just preaching to my congregation, I was preaching to myself. I allowed God to speak to me *and* through me.

I also intentionally took time to write things down. It forced me to process. Often, I would get stuck or pray about something and later on that day or week God would show up and reveal the way forward. So I began to write things down as they came to me in the notes app on my phone. This enables us to become more aware of our doubts and struggles in the moment while allowing us to reflect and learn from them later.

Going back to Groeschel's book, he says, "When I record it, it becomes a spiritual anchor that tethers me to God and to the consistency of God's promises."[14] God doesn't promise that there won't be difficulty, hardship, or bad times, but simply that He will *be there* during those times.

Finally, I took intentional time to meditate and pray. I'd wait until everyone was out of the house and off to school in the mornings so that I wouldn't face any distractions.

FAMILY

The greatest buffer we have for mental health is a good social structure. As Robin Roberts of *Good Morning America* likes to say, "Your tribe determines your vibe." Research confirms that support from friends and family is a key element in helping someone who is dealing with mental illness. It can provide a network of practical and emotional assistance. "Teamwork makes the dream work" may be a cheesy aphorism, but it fits and it's true for someone with mental health issues. They need a team, a caring team, surrounding them.

---

[14] Groeschel, p. 86

I was fortunate to have people around me who truly cared: my neighbor who came and sat with me on the floor while I was having a breakdown; my mom and dad who begged me to go get help; my wife who made the hard decision to take me to the mental hospital and who supported me when I got out. I had the support of the church council in my congregation. And I would be remiss if I didn't talk about my staff. They prayed for me, cared for me, and picked up the slack whenever I couldn't carry my weight. I owe *all* of them a debt of gratitude.

To have a tribe, you must tell them what's going on. Don't keep it inside. Part of the stigma of mental illness is that if we admit it we will look weak. We feel self-conscious about the way others see us, don't we? And for me, that was a *huge* part of it. How would I look as a husband, father, son, or pastor if people knew? Would my wife think less of me? Would my kids think less of me? Would my congregation lose faith in my leadership?

All of those questions revolve around the way we're perceived by the outside world and it's a stigma that we *must* overcome. Yes, it was hard having my family see me that way. Yes, it was embarrassing sitting on my floor crying my eyes out with my neighbor. Yes, it was humbling to tell my staff I had a problem and needed to get help. Yes, I was scared to death of how the congregation would react if they found out. In the end, they all reached out in love and care.

It can be scary when someone you love is sick. We know how to take care of people when they have the flu or a sinus infection or perhaps a stomach bug, but what do we do when they're having a mental health crisis? It's hard to see someone you love in pain. It can be confusing for kids to see dad or mom when they aren't acting like themselves. Someone struggling with mental illness needs extra love and care. Even though you may not be able to see the illness, it's there and you can help.

Learn the early warning signs of mental illness. Studies show that when the family is educated, the rate of people receiving help more than doubles. And that leads to the second thing you can do: encourage and assist them in seeking help. My wife went online and found a mental hospital. She made the call and pushed me to go. She knew I was in no mental state to decide for myself. Be their advocate (I'll touch more on being an advocate in the workplace in a later chapter).

Finally, continue to check in on them. Walk with them throughout their recovery. Support them in their counseling and in taking medications. When you do, the chances of them getting better only increase.

MEDITATION

Some of you may be surprised that meditation was one of the factors that helped me heal, but it's true. Look, I *never* thought I would be someone who could meditate. With my ADHD I figured there was no way I could sit still and concentrate for longer than two minutes at a time, and yet here I am. What I discovered is that there are a *lot* of misconceptions about meditation. I believed most of them.

In his book *Wherever You Go, There You Are*, author Jon Kabat-Zinn writes the following:

> *Meditation is simply about being yourself and knowing something about who that is. It is about coming to realize that you are on a path whether you like it or not, namely, the path that is your life. Meditation may help us see that this path we call our life has direction; that it is always unfolding, moment by moment; and that what happens now, in this moment, influences what happens next.* [15]

---

[15] Kabat-Zinn, Jon. *Wherever You Go, There You Are: Mindfulness Meditation In Everyday Life*. Hachette Books, 2010, p. 10

There's a joke in the meditation world that goes like this: "Don't just do something, sit there." But meditation isn't just about sitting; it's about *stopping*. It's about being present in the moment and learning from that moment in every way you can.

Meditation isn't something you get overnight. It takes practice, *consistent practice*. I also discovered that it's okay if your mind wanders. I didn't think we were *supposed* to let our minds wander; however, meditation involves becoming aware of that wandering mind and bringing it back to focus, "home base."

Home base is an image on which you can concentrate, one that brings good feelings to mind. For me, it's standing in our yard out on the farm and admiring the big oak tree in front of the pond. That image for me has "all the feels" (as they say). So whenever my mind starts to wander, I bring it back to *that* image—my home base. This creates muscle memory by training your brain to stay in the moment. Meditation taught me that the moment you're in is the most valuable moment of your life.

You can meditate anywhere. Yes, I have a meditation mat and pillow that I use daily. I use Apple Fitness Plus and their guided meditations, one of my own meditations (I'm certified in instructional meditation), or my Calm app. But I also meditate as I take my daily walks. How? By concentrating on being in *that* moment; by refusing to get caught up in the tasks of the day or the trials I might be going through; by paying attention to the trees, the leaves, the grass, the people passing by.

I meditated in the doctor's office the other day. I put in my earbuds, turned on some calming music, found my home base and stayed there. It was just a little embarrassing when I didn't hear them call my name and the nurse had to come tap me on the leg. But hey, what are you gonna do? In that moment, "when your mind becomes clear, empty, without being interrupted or disturbed by thoughts, the real mind comes to the front."[16]

---

[16] Williams, Michael. *Zen: Beginner's Guide to Understanding & Practicing Zen Meditation to Become Present.* 2017, p. 19

Meditation is known as the "Fundamental Practice" in the Zen/Buddhist world. It's easy to understand why. When you meditate, you can clear your mind of all negative emotions. You basically destroy their breeding ground, which allows your mind to become clear and allows you to incorporate gratitude and positivity into your life. So it wasn't just my Christian faith that helped me but also other faith traditions as well.

PHYSICAL HEALTH

I'm not the healthiest eater. One of the first things I needed to do was cut back on the amount of soda I was drinking. If you saw me at any point during the day, I probably had a Pepsi Max in my hand. At one point I was drinking between six and eight cans *per day*. I would even drink them late at night. I could chug a Pepsi before bed and still fall asleep as easily as switching off a light.

Well, it seemed as though my body was telling me that this wasn't going to be the case anymore, so I cut back dramatically on the amount of soda that I drank during the day. I now stick to around three, at most, and I always stop by 3:00 or 4:00 in the afternoon. After that, it is caffeine-free time for me. I must admit that it has helped my sleep habits dramatically.

Speaking of which, you're probably asking, "Hey Brad, how did you get a handle on your sleep issues without the medication?" Well, I went to a sleep doctor (which I didn't even know existed), and let me tell you, she has been a Godsend. I am also on some medication. I went to see this doctor early on after I stopped taking my previous prescriptions and explained everything that had happened and how the drugs had affected me both mentally and physically. I also explained the hypnic jerks, which she promised to investigate further.

In the meantime, I did a sleep study to ensure the problem wasn't sleep apnea. She also wanted to be certain that all the medication was out of my system by the time I came back to see her again. Folks, that sleep study was *crazy*. I had never been through one before, but by the time all those electrodes were attached to me, I thought there was no way I could fall asleep so there would be no way for them to get accurate results. I lay on the bed watching *The Big Bang Theory* and I remember thinking to myself, "I hope I don't choke myself in the middle of the night with all these wires!"

And then I slept the best I had in *weeks.*

With sleep apnea officially ruled out, my doctor did more research on my hypnic jerks and found evidence that increased magnesium intake might aid in regulating the neurotransmitters related to sleep and muscle relaxation. She wanted me to up my dosage to 500mg a day. She also prescribed a very low dose of a medication called Clonazepam, which has been known to help with both panic attacks and insomnia and may alleviate hypnic jerks as well. After that, I was falling asleep within 10 to 15 minutes.

I also began exercising more. I now walk around a mile and a half three days a week. The other days, I take Tae Kwon Do at my son's Do Jan. Adding exercise into your day has been proven to help with sleep. It certainly helped me! I had gotten used to sitting around the house on my computer all day without ever really moving around. The pandemic made things worse, with most of my meetings being on Zoom from my office. Exercising was a *huge* factor in getting me back into good physical health.

Lastly, as another adjustment to my diet, I started drinking a "greens" drink and taking a multivitamin to get the good stuff back into my system. Gut health is everything. Gut health *matters.* It affects every part of your body. Gut health also affects mental health because the gastrointestinal tract is very sensitive to emotion. The brain has a direct effect on the stomach and intestines (just think about how you sometimes feel nauseated when you're experiencing anxiety, stress, or trauma).[17] It's truly an intimate, symbiotic connection. Around 70% of the immune system is located within the walls of your gut.[18] I try to pay attention to my gut health as much as I can because it's *that* important.

EDUCATION

This may seem strange, but I went back to school. Yes, I started a certification program through Life Coach Jay Shetty. Jay founded his life coaching certification school a few years ago to help others discover their purpose and live their best lives now. I had read his book, *Think Like a Monk*, and I had to share it with the staff at church. We all read it together and when I saw the difference it made for them, I knew I needed to sign up for certification.

It wasn't just for me, though. I knew the lessons I'd learn would help me be a better pastor as well. I had been looking to improve in my areas of "counseling," so to speak. I place that word in quotations because pastors aren't certified counselors. We're a little like life coaches, but perhaps a better term would be a *spiritual guide*.

Jay's philosophy fit who I was. His purpose to make the world a better place by helping others live happier, more fulfilled lives was my purpose as well. I also came at it from a spiritual perspective, but I thought his teachings could help me to expand my reach beyond the church. Unfortunately, for many people church can be a painful place full of traumatic memories, but perhaps I could create a space where they were free to explore their faith and life without all the religious baggage. I also felt

---

[17] Kamiya, Atsushi. "The Brain-Gut Connection." Johns Hopkins Medicine, May 2019.

[18] Fields, Helen. "The Gut: Where Bacteria and Immune System Meet." Johns Hopkins Medicine, November 2015.

that my own history with ADHD and anxiety might enable me to more effectively coach others who may be dealing with similar struggles.

What I didn't realize was how much the courses would help me personally. As I went through each of the modules, I found my own path of healing. I used the principles and techniques I learned to help me heal from my mental struggles. They helped me become more aware of where I was. As I've said before, mindfulness is always the first step toward change and healing. I was able to do an audit of my life and begin setting goals for myself, along with building better habits and becoming consistent in those habits. It truly helped me to reflect and heal. Now I want to share that with others. This may seem like shameless self-promotion—so pardon the plug—but if you'd like to begin a journey of purpose and fulfillment, I'd love to be your guide. Visit my website, www.riseandstart.life, and let's get started today.

Identity

In 2005 my wife and I moved to Houston from Austin as newlyweds. It was shortly thereafter that my identity was stolen. I had gone to the local Wal-Mart to return one of our wedding gifts. The customer service agent told me she couldn't complete the return due to a bad check that I had allegedly written. *Bad check? What does she mean?* I asked if I could speak to a manager who said she would try her best to look into the situation, but there was only so much she could find out. I was okay with that.

Finally, after about half an hour of digging, all she could tell me was that there was a $1,500 check in my name that had bounced at a Wal-Mart in Austin, Texas. I asked when and as soon as she told me the date, I knew. There was no way that I could have written that bad check because we were on a cruise ship in the middle of the Caribbean for our honeymoon.

Obviously, I had a problem. Shortly thereafter, I began receiving collection notices in the mail for crazy amounts: $3,000 at Academy, $2,000 at Office Depot, and sure enough, that $1,500 at Wal-Mart. Someone had been forging checks to University Federal Credit Union, a bank which I had never used, and was using my information to go on a shopping spree. I needed Frank William Abagnale and I needed him now.[19] Instead, I called the police department, filed a report, and then I put a freeze on my credit reports.

It doesn't feel good to have your identity stolen. Have you

---

[19] If you don't know who that is, check out the 2002 film *Catch Me If You Can* starring Leonardo DiCaprio and Tom Hanks.

ever had that happen to you? I was weirded out by the whole experience. All I could do was picture someone out there walking around acting like me, doing all these illegal things in my name, and I had no control over any of it.

That's what my mental illness felt like at its peak. I felt like I was looking at my life from the outside in, seeing someone else living my life without any control over it. Like someone had hacked my Xbox game and was playing for me. While our identities may be tied to things like our driver's licenses or social security numbers, the truth is that our identities are far more multidimensional. Somehow, through all of this, I had lost mine and I needed to get it back.

Unfortunately, we tend to define ourselves by what society and others say about us. The more we allow ourselves to sink down that rabbit hole, the more lost and confused we become.

Daniel Day-Lewis is the only actor to win the Best Actor Oscar three times. Here's a quiz: How many times was he nominated? Six, giving him a 50% winning percentage. Not too shabby. So what makes him so good at what he does? He uses a technique called Method Acting which requires the actor to live as much like their character as possible in order to *become* the role the actor is playing. For instance, in *Gangs of New York*, he trained to be a butcher, spoke with a thick Irish accent on and off the set, and hired circus performers to teach him how to throw knives. He was also known to have walked around Rome in character in 19th-century clothing, starting fights with people on the streets. It's a grueling technique if you go all in and it can take its toll on an actor. Heath Ledger used this technique for his role as the Joker in *The Dark Knight*. It drove him into depression and ultimately cost him his life.

Unconsciously we are all method acting to some degree. We have the personas that we play at work, at home, online, and everywhere else, but in doing so, we wrap our identities around what other people think of us. For many of us, especially those who struggle with mental illness, it ends up being a devastating game.

In *Think Like a Monk,* Jay Shetty writes, "When we tune out the opinions, expectations, and obligations of others, we begin to hear ourselves."[20] I needed to listen to myself. I was asking the right questions: *Who am I? What is my purpose? What do I value? What do I want to do with my life?* I just wasn't listening to myself. I was listening to what the world was telling me. In the ancient Hindu text the Bhagavad Gita, the sage Vyasa writes, "It is better to live your own destiny imperfectly than to live an imitation of somebody else's life with perfection,"[21] or as sociologist Charles Cooley asks, "Am I who I think I am, or am I who others think I am?"[22]

Our stories begin at a very young age. All the places we go, all the people we meet, all the books we read, and all the emotions we experience help shape who we are. Where did you grow up? Did you live in hardship or a life of luxury? Where did you get your education? Whatever the answer, those elements of your upbringing have shaped your values. All these things slowly instill values within us whether we realize it or not. They don't just come to us in our sleep. We can't turn on a light switch and... *hey look, values!*

Often, we don't even think them through; they sit in our unconscious minds, subtly influencing our words, actions, and decisions. *Except when they don't.* I truly believe the only way to live your most authentic life is to live out your values. When we don't, those are the times when we feel lost and helpless.

When we're born, we are given a name. Our names have significance. They have power. They can even define us. In the ancient Near East, during Biblical times, your name was more

---

[20] Shetty, Jay. *Think Like a Monk: Train Your Mind for Peace and Purpose Every Day.* Simon & Schuster, 2020, p. 11

[21] Bhagavad Gita. Chapter 3, Verse 35

[22] Shetty, p. 3

than just a handful of letters pushed together; your name was your *identity*. Your name reflected your character, your soul, your very being. In essence, your name told others who you were.

I started a non-profit in 2014 that helps children in rural areas of Africa obtain an education by providing schools with supplies, books, buildings, and anything else they need. Over the years, my tour guide, Yohannes Wassie, has truly become my brother. I am an only child, so I consider him my brother from another mother. His family is my family and vice versa.

When his mother passed away he and his wife Zeni found out they were going to have a baby—my niece! Yohannes named her Selenat, which means "tribute to my mother" as he truly felt that this precious new life was a gift sent to him by his mom.

To be asked your name is literally to be asked: *Who are you?* Over the past several years in my struggle with mental illness, I had a hard time with that question. I felt as though I didn't know the answer anymore. I listened too much to the outside noise and not enough to my inner voice. It wasn't until I began to recognize the difference between that outside noise and my inner voice that change began to happen.

Jay Shetty talks a lot about how our values are influenced by whatever absorbs our minds. "We are not our minds," he writes, "but the mind is the vehicle by which we decide what is important in our hearts."[23] I was allowing social media, Hollywood, news articles, and society in general to tell me a certain story about mental illness. I foolishly allowed those voices to convince me that I was broken, that I was a failure, and that my life was over. I had given those thoughts permission to take up residence in my mind.

In order to begin figuring out who I was, I needed to do the hard work of figuring out my values. I knew they were there, but I never really thought to write them down. Rarely do we put such things into words. While it's indeed important for an

---

[23] Shetty, p. 10

organization to know its values, it is equally important for each individual to know their values and to live by them.

Values are the attitudes and behaviors that we exhibit. They are the moral code by which we live. They are the threads that weave together the tapestry of who we are. Values can become your moral compass. Just as a compass can point us in the right direction, our values do the same. They are the drivers of our lives.

Through my journey, I've also discovered that knowing our values can contribute to our mindfulness. Values also help us set priorities, assist in decision making, and allow us to take an assessment of our lives. If you are struggling with where to start, I would encourage you to head to the LEAD organization's website, www.waytolead.org/values-cards, where they provide a special deck of cards that can help you begin to determine your values.

Another way to determine your values is to use a list I discovered in a story Jay Shetty tells in *Think Like a Monk*. The story is about a time in the *ashram* (a monastic community) when his teacher explained the difference between higher and lower values. Higher values propel and elevate us toward happiness, fulfillment, and meaning, while lower values demote us toward anxiety, depression, and suffering.

According to the Bhagavad Gita, the higher values are fearlessness, purity of mind, gratitude, service and charity, acceptance, performing sacrifice, deep study, austerity, straightforwardness, nonviolence, truthfulness, absence of anger, renunciation, perspective, restraint from fault-finding, compassion toward all living beings, satisfaction, gentleness/kindness, integrity, and determination. Jay points out in his book that happiness and success are *not* included on that list because they are goals or rewards, not values.[24]

Then he goes on to describe the six lower values in the

---

[24] Shetty, p. 15-16

Bhagavad Gita: greed, lust, anger, ego, illusion, and envy. Yes, only six. His teacher at the ashram pointed out that there are always more ways to be pulled up than to be pulled down. Somehow, we allow those six things to pull us down and we forget about the higher values. For me, I used the higher value list to form my values: gratitude, service and charity, compassion, and integrity. You might remember from the beginning of my journey that I felt like my integrity was being called into question and how I felt the judicatory leader hadn't approached our conversation with caring (or perhaps I should call it *compassion*). Both integrity and compassion are important elements of my value set.

Find a time to give yourself space and stillness to ponder who you are. When we give ourselves this space, we can then begin to clean the cobwebs away and truly see ourselves for who we are and not how others see us. I encourage you to identify your values and begin to let them guide your life. If you need guidance on how to do that, you know where to find me.

No Matter What Else, at Least You're You

Forgiveness is hard. Alexander Pope said, "To err is human, to forgive is divine." It's something that doesn't come naturally to us. We would rather get revenge or pretend it didn't happen. Often we practice what I call "Band-Aid forgiveness," which is when we believe we have forgiven but we really haven't. Band-Aids cover up wounds but they don't heal. This type of forgiveness hides but never heals the wound.

It's hard enough to forgive others, but what about ourselves? I had to do some soul-searching, to be honest, and I was having a very hard time forgiving myself for what I put my family, friends, and staff at church through. Sure, they told me all the right things: *I forgive you. It's not your fault. It's something you couldn't help.* But I still felt this overwhelming sense of guilt. In my head, I knew they were right, but deep down in my soul, I was downright angry with myself.

Now, I don't think we can ever get through life without feeling regret at some point, it's a completely normal reaction. However, our *response* to regret and guilt can often cause problems. If I couldn't find a way to forgive myself, I was going to end up right back where I started.

As author Alona Bishop points out in her book *How to Forgive Yourself,* guilt that's left unchecked can be incredibly harmful. "When not acted upon in a productive way, it can cause problems with our physical and mental health. Ongoing, intense feelings of guilt are a major source of chronic stress. Chronic stress can result in anxiety disorders, trouble sleeping, depression, heart disease, digestive issues, and a weakened immune system."[25] I certainly didn't need any of *that*. I was just getting back to sleeping well and I didn't want a relapse of the anxiety disorder that I seemed to have under control, so I needed to find a way to forgive myself.

The first step was to accept that the past is the past and there isn't a damn thing I can do to change it. That's the thing, isn't it? We can't control the future, and we can't change the past, so all we have is the present. We *do* have a choice as to how we'll live each moment. We have control over what we let in and what we don't. We can decide to change our thought patterns about past events.

And *that* was the second step: changing my thought patterns about what had happened. As Alona Bishop writes, "When we are unable to forgive ourselves, it is because we hold onto negative thoughts associated with certain events."[26] I was holding on to the negative thoughts regarding my panic attacks and my anxiety, and I needed to change the way that I looked at those events because that point of view was extremely limited.

What would happen if I looked at them from a positive standpoint? So I began to journal and ask myself certain questions: What good came from those difficult moments? What have I learned about myself? Am I a better person now than I was then?

I learned that when you change the way you look at things, the things you look at begin to change.

We have to learn to treat life as a classroom—always a place to learn. And I've learned the most during times when I wasn't my

---

[25] Bishop, Alona. *How to Forgive Yourself: A Step by Step Guide to Forgiving Yourself and Letting Go of the Past.* CreateSpace Independent Publishing, 2015, Location No. 33
[26] Bishop, Location No. 122

best. What good came out of these past several years? I believe
that I became closer to my family and my understanding of *family*
deepened.

"Families stick together" became more than a clichéd
aphorism; I got to see it firsthand. I saw my wife stick by the vows
we made on the day we got married: *For better or worse, in sickness
and in health*. And then there were the small things: I learned I
had high blood pressure that would have gone undetected had I
not been forced to make an appointment with a cardiologist, I've
learned meditation and the value that it brings to people's lives,
and I've learned to become more aware of my emotions and how
to deal with them.

Am I better today than I was two years ago? *Absolutely*. Do I
still have a ways to go? *Undoubtedly*. As Alona Bishop writes, "You
will always be more aware today than you were yesterday. Just as
it is not fair to judge a child from the perspective of an adult, it
is not fair to judge yesterday's version of you with the awareness
that you have today."[27]

LEARNING TO LOVE MYSELF

"This kind of compulsive concern with 'I, me, and mine' isn't
the same as loving ourselves… Loving ourselves points us to
capacities of resilience, compassion, and understanding within
that are simply part of being alive."[28]

I have mixed emotions about Valentine's Day. I always feel
pressured. Do you feel that? I mean, I feel pressured into showing
love to the people I love on this one day of the year when in
actuality I should be showing that love to them every day. Walk
into a grocery store on February 13th and you will see more

---

[27] Bishop, Location No. 198
[28] Salzberg, Sharon. *The Force of Kindness: Change Your Life with Love
and Compassion*. Sounds True, 2010, p. 85-102

Valentine's Day paraphernalia than you ever do for Halloween. *Honestly.* It's more of a money-making scheme than anything if you ask me. Granted, I still buy my wife a card and a gift (same with my mom), but I *really* ought to be more concerned with showing them love each and every day.

Do you know who else you should show some love to every day? *Yourself.* If there's one person we have a hard time loving, it's the person we see in the mirror each day. Why is it easier to love others than to love ourselves? Sometimes we are truly *awful* to ourselves. We can be our own worst critics and spend inordinate amounts of time dwelling on our inadequacies. Amid my mental health struggles, I was my own worst critic. I needed to find a way to love myself again, even amidst my flaws and shortcomings.

Loving yourself isn't selfish. How can you love others if you don't know how to love the person you're closest to? You are the *only* person who will always be with you until the day you die. The longest relationship in your life is always with yourself, so start loving *you.*

So how do we do that?

Know Yourself.

Who are you? We've already discussed this in the previous chapter on identity, so I won't spend much time on it here but take some time to ponder this question: *Who am I?* Look at your values, what you're passionate about, and the areas in which you excel. Start there; live out your values and passions.

Stop comparing yourself to others.

For years I subscribed to *Men's Health* magazine. I would look at the dudes on the cover and tell myself, "Yep, get yourself in shape. Look like that!" I would go all out. I'd head down to the Vitamin shop, buy the latest and greatest supplements, and then start working out. Most of the time, it lasted for about a week... maybe two. I would backslide for a while and then another magazine would come. My wife would mention the huge arm muscles of the guy on the cover and I was off to the gym once again.

Somewhere along the line I just stopped. I stopped reading it and I stopped trying so hard. I didn't have to look like them. My dad-bod rocked and my wife loved me no matter what. I also had a habit of comparing what we had to what our neighbors had and I'll tell you something, keeping up with the Joneses is exhausting work. I would not advise it one bit.

Then I would compare myself to other pastors: *Oh look at what he's doing. Oh, wow, look how successful he's become.* And that is *just* as exhausting. I needed to be me. That's it. Period. And you have to be you. Remember, you have value just as you are. Comparison will constantly cloud the call God has on your life. Please, read that last sentence again and make it your mantra. Say it to yourself as many times as you need to hear it.

Stop listening to what the world says you are.

One of my favorite song lyrics comes from "Chasing Cars" by Snow Patrol: "If I just lay here, would you lie with me and just forget the world? I need your grace to remind me to find my own."[29] *You find your own.* I had to stop listening to what the world was telling me regarding my mental health.

I also had to stop listening to what the world was saying about what I had to be as a pastor—always put together, never struggling, always smiling, never angry with anyone... you get the idea. The list could go on and on. I had to remember that I was my own person. I lived out being a pastor in my own way and that was okay. Once I got real with myself, I started loving myself again. And once I got real about who I was as a

---

[29] Lightbody, Gary; Jonathan Quinn, Natah Connolly, Paul Wilson, Tom Simpson. *Eyes Open.* Interscope Records, 2006.

pastor, I started preaching with more authenticity and my love for ministry returned.

Learn to say no when you need to.

One thing I'm still not very good at is saying "no" when I need to. During my struggles, I was not protecting my calendar—and therefore my time with my family. I allowed my work to encroach on my family time and it wasn't healthy. There's this idea that pastors have to be "on" 24/7. And yes, while we need to be available to the people with whom we are entrusted, it shouldn't come at the expense of our families or our health.

Let's face it, the people in the pews will prioritize *their* families as well. How do I know this? Because every Sunday people choose activities or sports or staying home with their families over the church. Here's something we can all learn: *It's okay to say no.* I know it's hard because we don't want to disappoint people, but when we start saying yes to *everyone*, the next thing we know our calendars are full and our anxiety starts to rise.

We somehow think that by saying no we will lose out on opportunities and additional chances in the future. But a key challenge is prioritizing the opportunities that come so that you can be more successful when you *do* say yes. And it doesn't have to be a cold, flat-out no. You can decline something gently, explaining why, and I guarantee you that people will be significantly more understanding.

By saying no, we are prioritizing our own deadlines, needs, and desires, and it is an important step on the road to self-care and better mental health. Saying no is one of the most self-empowering things you can do. According to the Harvard Business Review, "success in [choosing not to pursue an opportunity] is founded on the ability to manage the emotions that come up when we close a door or extinguish an option."[30]

Be present.

This is a tough one. In today's consumer-driven culture, we oftentimes find ourselves overwhelmed. It can be truly hard to be present in the moment. I am reminded of one of Paul's letters to the Corinthians in which he tells the church, "Don't be wishing you were someplace else or with someone else, where you are right now is God's place for you. Live and obey and love and believe right there."[31] *Love and believe right there.* Love yourself right there. Believe in yourself right there. Where you are right now is where God has placed you, so be fully present so you don't miss out on what God has in store for you.

Your presence matters. My presence mattered to my family. Why was I engulfing myself in all the nonsense that was going on at the church? I wasn't fully present at the campsite right before my huge meltdown and I hadn't been fully present in the months that led up to that event. I missed out and those are months I won't get back.

I am trying to be fully present in each moment that I find myself in now. Here I am writing a book about my mental health journey and yet *this* is where God has placed me. The great theologian Frederick Buechner once said, "The place God calls you to is the place where your deep gladness and the world's hunger meet." One of the reasons I started practicing meditation was so that I could train my brain to be fully present in each moment. Remember, it's possible to be there and not really be *there.*

---

[30] Batista, Ed. "Learning to Say 'No' Is Part of Success." *Harvard Business Review*, November 2013.
[31] Holy Bible, 1 Corinthians 7:17 (*The Message*)

Treat Yourself.

I'm not going to draw this one out. We need to stop and have fun occasionally. So go out and do things. Rest. Read a book. Take a vacation. Make some time for *you*.

Give yourself a break when you make mistakes.

You are probably harder on yourself than anyone else. Cut yourself some slack. Mistakes are going to happen. You aren't going to be "on" every minute of the day. You can't be perfect all the time. After all, it's those little imperfections that make you great.

In studying the Buddhist way of living, every author I've read has emphasized the importance of compassion; however, it never occurred to me that I should not only have compassion for others but also for myself. I have spent the last 16 years of my life teaching people in my congregations to show love and compassion for our neighbors, yet I never even considered the idea of turning that compassion inward.

From the Buddhist view, you have to care about yourself before you can begin to care for others. As Kristin Neff writes in her book, *Self Compassion*, "If you are continually judging and criticizing yourself while trying to be kind to others, you are drawing artificial boundaries and distinctions that only lead to feelings of separation and isolation."[32]

Folks, that is the opposite of universal love because the universe includes *you*.

---

[32] Neff, Kristin. *Self-Compassion: The Proven Power of Being Kind to Yourself.* Yellow Kite, 2011, p. 189

The Mental Health Crisis in the United States

I am writing this chapter in June of 2022. Already this year, five celebrities have committed suicide: Hollywood manager Chris Huvane, Miss USA Chelsie Kryst, MLB player Jerry Giambi, country music legend Naomi Judd, and Peter Robbins, the voice of Charlie Brown. Those are just a few that I know off the top of my head because they're all "notable." But what about the people we *don't* hear about?

We see the numbers, but behind every number is a story and I truly believe that everybody is somebody. We have a major problem in the United States when it comes to mental health. There are thousands more who die by suicide, millions who attempt suicide, and millions more who struggle with mental health. All of whom go unnoticed by the media, so their stories are never heard.

According to the World Health Organization, almost seven hundred thousand people die by suicide every year.[33] And according to the American Foundation for Suicide Prevention, in 2020 alone, 45,979 people died by suicide—that's 130 suicides per day. It is the third leading killer among 10 to 19-year-olds, the second leading cause of death among 20 to 34-year-olds, and the rate is highest among middle-aged white men. Suicide is the

---

[33] Suicide Fact Sheet. *World Health Organization*, June 2021, www.who. int/news-room/fact-sheets/detail/suicide

biggest killer of men under the age of 50. That puts the male suicide rate at 3.9 times higher than females.[34]

As I write those statistics, my head is shaking. I feel a bit of anger welling up inside of me. Two glaring things stick out to me: First, suicide is the leading killer among 10 to 19-year-olds. We need to become more aware of what is happening with our kids. Parents, it's time to put down the phones and iPads and begin talking to our children about their lives and what they're feeling. We need to create spaces where our children feel safe discussing their struggles and vulnerabilities.

Second, I look at those statistics and see myself right in the bullseye. I am a middle-aged white male. Those numbers tell me that not only do we need to end the stigma of mental health, but we need to end the stigma of "manning up". This form of masculinity is toxic; we're killing ourselves.

As boys, we are told to be brave. There is immense pressure to be competitive, strong, and tough. There is a need to win, for emotional control and risk-taking. I have seen it in the interactions between my son, who is currently seven years old, and the kids in our neighborhood. My son is a lot like his dad—he wears his emotions on his sleeve. When he isn't seen as tough or strong or competitive, other kids seem to look down on him. *And it hurts.* It hurts me because I know it's hurting him.

Joel Wong, who conducted an Indiana University Bloomington study on the relationship between conformity to masculine stereotypes and mental health, reports: "In general, individuals who conformed strongly to masculine norms tend to have poorer mental health and less favorable attitudes toward

---

[34] Suicide Statistics. *American Foundation for Suicide Prevention,* February 2022, www.afsp.org/suicide-statistics

seeking psychological help..."[35] Men, it's time to let go of the cliché of "toughing it out."

I tried that and I ended up in a mental hospital. For the first time, there was a moment I thought of ending it all. We need to find *true* strength in showing vulnerability and stop faking the macho bullshit. I found a company in the United Kingdom called *Boys Get Sad Too*. Their mission is to open conversations around mental health by acknowledging the fact that it affects everyone and that it's okay for men to show emotion.

So what about mental health care? We were already struggling in this area before the pandemic hit. According to Mental Health America, 19.86% of adults experienced mental illness, which is the equivalent of nearly 50 million people. Moreover, 10.6% of the youth in America suffer from major depression, roughly 2.5 million kids. The numbers are even higher (14.5%) among kids who identify as more than one race.[36]

Perhaps most staggering of all is the percentage of adults and youth with a mental illness who report unmet treatment needs. According to a recent article in Forbes magazine, 45% of adults with a mental illness do not seek professional help[37] and over 60% of youth with major depression never receive treatment.[38] In my home state of Texas,[39] we rank at the bottom, nearly three-quarters of youth who struggle with depression never receive any kind of mental health care.

Why aren't people seeking help? Let's go back to the second chapter of this book. Remember my struggles with trying to find

---

[35] "Study Finds Sexism May Be Harmful to Men's Mental Health." Indiana University Bloomington, December 2016, education.indiana. edu/news/2016/2016-12-15-wong

[36] Reinert, M, Fritze, D. & Nguyen, T. "The State of Mental Health in America 2022." *Mental Health America*, October 2021, p. 27

[37] Nietzel, Michael. "Almost Half of Americans Don't Seek Professional Help For Mental Disorders." *Forbes*, May 2021.

[38] Reinert, p. 8

[39] Reinert, p. 32

a psychiatrist who would take my insurance? If it wasn't covered I'd have to pay out of pocket. The highest cost I was told was $250 per visit and the lowest was $300 a month. In the same Forbes article I mentioned previously, they included the top five reasons why people don't seek help. Affordability rounds out the list.

Another one of the top reasons was a lack of knowledge of what kind of help to seek or where to get it. During my breakdown in early September 2020, my wife had no idea where to turn. I had been to the emergency room several times, but as you may remember, none of them gave me the help I needed. It was a dose of morphine to calm me down and then they sent me on my way. Is it any wonder that the number-two reason people don't seek help is because of a lack of confidence in mental health treatment? The final reason, of course, is the stigma surrounding mental health and the fear of exposure.

The implications of these findings raise an important question: While we may overcome the stigma of mental health, are we concentrating enough on the actions taken once a mental illness is revealed? Why do so many Americans lack confidence or knowledge in getting help? Is it the media coverage? Let's face it… whenever mental illness is discussed, it usually follows a mass school shooting, the tragic death of some movie star, or explosive violence by some online influencer.

Sure, the stigma surrounding mental health may not be the *primary* reason why people don't seek help, but I think we would be doing ourselves a disservice by simply dismissing it. The aforementioned report by Forbes, using the Mental Health Quotient, leaves open the possibility that people may simply claim they prefer self-help over professional care because they worry about the social repercussions.

Part of my reason for writing this book is to show people that there is nothing to fear. And yes, while I *am* petrified about laying myself bare, I believe talking about my mental health struggles can do a lot of good by revealing that even a person who may seem to "have it all together" can suffer just the same. It's time to stop telling people, "Pull yourself together. You have a great life." That doesn't help. I'm also writing this to expose the cracks that exist in both the American healthcare system and in the Church as a whole.

So what can we do?

I honestly believe all of us can help in some way or another. We previously discussed how to have a caring conversation with someone who is struggling with mental health. Allow me to repeat it here:

- Listen without making judgments and concentrate on their needs in that moment
- Ask them what would help them
- Avoid confrontation
- Ask if there is someone they would like you to contact
- Let them know you are there for them

If you lead a company, a staff, or a team, begin to take the mental health of the people you work with seriously. Consider bringing on a life coach for your organization (by the way, I think I may know one). Create a budget line item to invest in the mental well-being of your people.

I've also been working on ways to make meetings more mindful. A few of these include:

- **Do a self-check-in before the meeting.** You're the team leader. Check your emotions, take a minute to breathe, and leave past baggage from previous meetings behind.
- **Conduct a one- or two-minute meditation before the meeting starts.** It can be a time of quiet with soft music. Allow everyone to leave behind their baggage and bring their minds into the meeting.
- **Go around the table and do a group check-in.** Highs and lows are always a good start.

- **Encourage an atmosphere that accepts clarifying questions.** This stops finger pointing and shaming in meetings and can also eliminate confusion and clear up expectations and intent.
- **Create a negative-free zone.** Most of the time we react negatively instead of with compassion. You may not agree with what a person says but accept their position and respect who they are.

Become a mental health advocate. I recently took my son to Six Flags. On the trip, I bought him a Superman cape. When he put it on he said, "Now I'm a superhero!" Well, not all heroes wear capes, but you can be a hero by advocating for those who cannot advocate for themselves. Talk to your boss at work about investing in the mental health and well-being of the employees. Explain that when the employees are healthy both physically and mentally, there's a better work environment, there's an increase in production, and there's far less employee turnover.

Encourage your local politicians to make mental health a priority. Every politician, no matter the party affiliation, *loves* to tout mental health after a crisis (especially mass shootings). As I was writing this chapter, 18 innocent elementary school children were gunned down in Uvalde, Texas, close to where I live, and all I have heard from our elected leaders is that we have to do a better job with mental health. We hear this *every time*, yet nothing gets done.

It was easier for an 18-year-old dropout to purchase two weapons and ammo than it was for me to see a psychiatrist. Do you notice the disparity here? It's time to *hold them accountable*. I see a whole lot of talking, but I don't see a whole lot of investment. Correct those who use stigmatizing language. It doesn't help. Education is important.

Finally, let's start making mental health a priority in our schools. Tend to the mental health needs of our teachers and our children. Destigmatize the discussion of mental health issues. Take time to practice breathing exercises before classes begin. Train counselors and coaches to understand mental health issues so that they're ready and able to discuss them with both students and teachers as needed.

As parents, we also need to talk about mental health more with our children. Remember the story about my grandfather going off to get help? That was the first time I had *ever* heard that story in my 43 years. I had no idea that my grandfather struggled with mental health issues. I *did* know about my grandparents' struggles with cancer, heart disease, and blood pressure. Why? Because those things were acceptable to talk about.

We tend to avoid any discussions of mental health. I'm not blaming my mom at all, but I'm mentioning this here because I feel it's important for us to discuss these issues with our families— that includes children. It's common for us to avoid talking to kids about mental illness to protect them from stress and confusion. Yes, there was a reason we chose to hide my mental breakdown from our children at the time, but as I have progressed in my healing, I realize that it's important to discuss my symptoms with my own kids.

My daughter has already shown signs of anxiety. In discussing my struggles with her, she was able to understand that she isn't alone and that dad knows what she's going through. But like they say in those airplane safety demonstrations, it is important to put on your oxygen mask first before you can help your child. Tend to yourself first and get to a good place; then you will be able to talk more openly and freely to them about your circumstances.

I can't tell you what age is a good time for you to begin discussing those conversations, but you'll know when the time is right, just like I did with my daughter. Either way, the best way to support your children and family is to lovingly help them understand your mental illness and its symptoms.

THE CLERGY HEALTH CRISIS

"Well, you only work one day a week. What can possibly be so bad?" Ugh... how often have I heard *that*? If I had a quarter for every time I did, my pension account would be in a lot better shape than it is now. Often, those words are meant as a joke, but deep down, we as clergy know that it holds a grain of truth. After all, people only see us on Sundays, they rarely see the work that we do during the week.

According to a study by the Clergy Health Initiative at Duke Divinity School,[40] a pastors' sense of guilt regarding not doing enough at work was a top predictor of depression and often leads to doubting their call to ministry, which was their top predictor of anxiety. Another factor that was found to be a powerful predictor of depression and anxiety was job stress. Clergy engage in numerous stressful activities, including grief counseling, navigating the competing demands of congregants, and delivering a weekly sermon that's always open to criticism. The strain of these roles is further amplified by having to switch rapidly between them.

A recent study published by *The Living Church* reveals that the clergy depression rate before the pandemic was 11.1% and the anxiety rate was 13.5%. Those are both twice the national average, and again, that's *before* the pandemic. In the Evangelical Lutheran Church in America (ELCA), the congregational body of which I am a part, 16% of clergy were treated for mental health disorders in the first half of 2020, which was an increase of 6.1% from the previous year. Furthermore, a full 20% of

---

[40] Proeschold-Bell, R.J., Miles, A., Toth, M. et al. "Using Effort-Reward Imbalance Theory to Understand High Rates of Depression and Anxiety Among Clergy." *The Journal of Primary Prevention*, 2013.

Protestant clergy rate their mental and emotional well-being as below average or poor.[41]

No doubt the pandemic has exacerbated these issues, along with the growing divide of political opinions on how to deal with that pandemic, resulting in clergy that are frankly burned out. Notably, in 2021 alone, there was a dramatic increase in the number of pastors who were thinking of giving up on ministry entirely.

I have witnessed this firsthand in the various clergy Facebook groups that I frequent. Pastors are on the verge of quitting because they are tired of getting beaten up over politics, face masks, or whether or not to have in-person services. According to a study by the Barna Group,[42] nearly two-in-five pastors have considered quitting full-time ministry, which would be 38% of the pastors in America. That number is highest among pastors under the age of 45, where it jumps up to 46%. The report also identifies another notable gap, "with pastors from mainline denominations far more likely to consider quitting than those from non-mainline denominations (51%-34% respectively)."

So what can the *church* do?

First of all, we *must* take the mental health of our clergy more seriously. In the ELCA, we have departments for youth, young adults, world hunger, and disaster response, yet no department for mental health. We have a "health" department, but they solely focus on insurance. We need the national Church to start educating our congregations regarding the mental health of clergy and to be an advocate for our ministers.

Our insurance for mental health must change. Six visits a year is not cutting it. It *must* be covered, and if we can't make more progress on the national level, then we need to do more on

---

[41] MacDonald, G. Jeffrey. "Stress Compounded for Clergy in Pandemic." *The Living Church*, November 2020.
[42] "38% of U.S. Pastors Have Thought About Quitting Full-Time Ministry in the Past Year." *Barna*, November 2021.

the local level instead. If you are a member of a church, please encourage your congregation to create a mental health budget for your pastor. Most of us have continuing education budgets because a leader who isn't growing isn't able to lead a growing organization, but a mental health budget is equally important. It can help cover the costs insurance doesn't, it can help cover costs of spiritual coaching, it can provide for meditation classes, or it can even pay for supplements or prescriptions for mental health issues. Moreover, when the door is opened for your pastor to receive the proper care when it's needed, it sends a message that the congregation truly cares about their mental and emotional well-being.

On a local level, we can also create a mental health team for the pastor. This could be a group of individuals in the congregation that ensures the pastor is taking time away for themselves; that they are using their vacation days; that they are getting the help they need if they are struggling with mental illness. Another option would be for your congregation to create a policy that allows a pastor who is struggling with mental illness to be given an extended time away to concentrate on getting the help they need without any repercussions or penalties for doing so.

Churches talk about compassion *a lot*. So when it comes to the mental health of their spiritual leaders, this is an area in which the Church can begin to live out that compassion. Your pastor isn't someone you don't know, someone who lives across the world, or the latest charity case. Your pastor is your spiritual leader. How can we expect them to feed and nurture their communities if they aren't being fed and nourished themselves?

Who Lives, Who Dies, Who Tells Your Story

The poet Yung Pueblo wrote that inner peace isn't about feeling perfect all the time or not caring about what is happening; rather, it's about being with your emotions without reacting to them; it's the calmness that emerges when you embrace change.[43] *He's right.* I've had to change many aspects of my life, but all those changes were for the better. In this final chapter, I want to examine five stages to finding your inner peace.

DON'T BE AFRAID OF CHANGE

We hate change. It's often scary and it rarely comes easy. Most of us spend a great deal of time and energy trying to avoid change, but the truth is that we can't run from it forever. As discussed throughout this book, I've had to change several things in my life to discover my path to healing. And while you'd think I might welcome it due to my ADHD, change has been pretty difficult.

Any alteration of my routine puts me into a fit of sorts, but learning to cope with change, rather than being afraid of it, lowers the risk of anxiety and depression. So embrace change, especially change for the better, and don't allow yourself to be ruled by fear.

---

[43] Pueblo, p. 174

BE HONEST WITH YOURSELF

We are taught at a young age that honesty is the best policy. When my two children get in trouble, I always encourage them that telling the truth is better than getting caught in a lie.

I had lied to myself for a long time. I had to wake up and be honest with the man in the mirror. *I was not okay.* A person can be honest with the entire world, but if they're not honest with themselves, none of it really matters. If I had been honest with myself, I would have admitted sooner that I needed help. If I had been honest with myself, I would not have worried so much about who others thought I should be—as both a pastor and as a man—and instead stayed true to the person God created me to be.

I have found that it is easier to be honest with others than with yourself. By finally being honest with myself, I cast off fear and self-doubt; I gained clarity; my relationships became healthier; life became more beautiful. I stopped stressing as much and have been able to take things as they come. And that, my friends, is a beautiful thing.

MINDFULNESS

I've talked about mindfulness before, but it really did represent a seismic shift in my life. The entire concept of mindfulness—a Western version of meditation—has only been around for about 50 years or so and it was created for the purpose of living life in the Western world today.

In this fast-paced world, it enables us to experience less stress and less anxiety, feel more peaceful, and deal with pain and illness (both mental and physical). Practicing mindfulness has truly helped me connect with the simple moments in life by living in the current *now.* Whenever I do, it becomes possible to discover a sense of peace and state of alert, focused relaxation, and enjoyment—to experience life as it unfolds.

This was the problem that led to that first huge meltdown. In order to experience true inner peace, being mindful helps us cultivate a true appreciation for the fullness of each moment we are alive. Wherever you go, be truly there!

SERVICE TOWARD OTHERS

Kindness matters. According to an article published by the Mental Health Foundation in the United Kingdom,[44] evidence shows that helping others can also benefit our own mental health and well-being by reducing stress, improving mood, self-esteem, and a sense of happiness. Contrary to popular belief, you don't have to own anything in order to serve. Good deeds often take little time or cost any money. As Jay Shetty writes in *Think Like a Monk*, "Selflessness is the surest route to inner peace and a meaningful life. Selflessness heals the self."[45]

The simple act of compassion and serving others has been linked to increased feelings of well-being.[46] In my work overseas with my non-profit organization, I also discovered that helping others can change our perspective. Many people don't realize the impact a different perspective can have on their outlook on life.

Sister Christine Vladimiroff, a Benedictine nun, once said, "Monastic spirituality teaches us that we are on a journey. The journey is inward to seek God in prayer and silence. Taken alone, we can romanticize this aspect of our life... but to be monastic

---

[44] "Kindness Matters Guide." Mental Health Foundation, United Kingdom, October 2020.
[45] Shetty, p. 256
[46] Curry, Oliver Scott; Lee Rowland, Caspar Van Lissa, et al. "Happy to help? A systematic review and meta-analysis of the effects of performing acts of kindness on the well-being of the actor." *Journal of Experimental Social Psychology*, 2018.

there is a parallel journey—the journey outward. We live in community to grow in sensitivity to the needs of others... the monastery is then a center to come out of and to invite others into. The key is always to maintain both journeys—inward and outward."[47]

Likewise, the path to inner peace is not only inward but it is also outward.

BE GRATEFUL

The word "gratitude" is derived from the Latin *gratia*, which can refer to grace, graciousness, or gratefulness, and, in some ways, gratitude encompasses each of those definitions. Benedictine monk Brother David Steindl-Rast defines gratitude as "the feeling of appreciation when you recognize that something is valuable to you, which has nothing to do with monetary worth."[48] One thing that I learned through my life coaching certification was to encourage clients to begin each day in gratitude. And if I was going to encourage my clients to do that, I figured I needed to as well. So now I begin each day by saying out loud what I am grateful for.

Gratitude has been linked to better mental health. According to a recent article published by Harvard Medical School, a pair of psychologists who were researching gratitude asked the participants in their study to write a few sentences each week focused on specific topics: "One group wrote about things they were grateful for that had occurred during the week. A second group wrote about daily irritations or things that had displeased them, and the third wrote about events that had affected them (without a positive or negative emphasis). After 10 weeks, those

---

[47] Ward, Hannah. *The Monastic Way: Ancient Wisdom for Contemporary Living*. Wm. B. Eerdmans Publishing, 2007.
[48] Shetty, p. 213

who wrote about gratitude were more optimistic and felt better about their lives. Surprisingly, they also exercised more and had fewer visits to physicians than those who had focused on sources of aggravation."[49]

Also, according to UCLA neuroscientist Alex Korb, we can't truly focus on positive and negative feelings at the same time: "When we feel grateful, our brains release dopamine (the reward chemical), which makes us want to feel that way again, and we begin to make gratitude a habit. Once you start seeing things to be grateful for, your brain starts looking for more things to be grateful for. It's a virtuous cycle."[50]

Wake up each day and begin that day with gratitude. Write down everything that makes you grateful. If that's too much, write "What are you grateful for today?" on a sticky note and put it right where you'll see it as soon as you roll out of bed. If you do that instead of reaching for your cell phone first thing in the morning, you'll be doing your mental health a huge favor and you can begin down the path toward inner peace.

In fact, you will soon find yourself seeking out things to be grateful for instead of focusing on the negative. Helen Keller once wrote, "When one door of happiness closes, another opens, but often we look so long at the closed door that we do not see the one which has been opened for us."[51]

[49] "Giving thanks can make you happier." *Harvard Health Publishing*, August 2021.
[50] Korb, Alex. "The Grateful Brain: The neuroscience of giving thanks." *Psychology Today*, November 2012.
[51] Keller, Helen. *We Bereaved*. Leslie Fulenwider, Inc., 1929.

Afterword

This is my story. It may not be yours, but it's mine. As I wrote in the introduction, you don't have to be proud of your story, but you do have to *own* it. I have come this far and have begun a journey to find inner peace. Have I found it yet? Well... *somewhat.* I can see glimmers of it here and there, but the important part is that I *am* finding it again.

I can feel my purpose and drive, which were once lost, beginning to come back. I am content. On one of my podcasts, I was interviewing my friend and colleague Pastor Chris Markert (who wrote the Foreword to this book). In that interview, we were discussing mental health. He said something so profound it truly gave me pause: "There's a difference between healing and being cured."

As I sat with that for a few days, I realized he was right. Healing and curing are inherently different. Curing means "eliminating all evidence of disease." A bladder infection can be cured. The flu can be cured. Even cancer can be cured. All can be treated with medicine and can be eliminated.

But I can't eliminate anxiety. I can't eliminate ADHD. They will *always* be a part of me. So while I can't be cured, I absolutely *can* continue toward healing. After all, healing is about "becoming whole." The *becoming* means that you are always on the way to that wholeness. Will we ever get there? I'd like to think so, but we must accept the journey.

As a Christian, I am reminded of the Resurrection of Christ. Jesus rose from the dead after three days in the tomb, and yet his wounds were still there, still visible, for all his disciples to see.

Those wounds are a part of him, just like our wounds are a part of us. However, that doesn't mean resurrection can't happen and it *certainly* doesn't mean those wounds have to define us. To that end, curing involves the physical realm while healing comes at a spiritual and emotional level. Being cured sometimes has an end in sight, while healing seems to be an ongoing process. And *that* is exactly where I am.

My hope in writing this book is that we begin to see mental health in a different light and that it is but one small chapter of a greater, grander story; that we end the stigmatization around mental health and begin to take the treatment of mental illness more seriously; that we not only talk about it but that our words lead to action.

My hope in writing this book is that people with mental health issues see their illness as just a *part* of their story, not something that defines who they are. That they would see that they are not alone and, like me, there are people around them who are ready to help.

There's a song that was written for Disney's *Dream Big, Princess* project called "Live Your Story," and that is what I want to leave you with. If you're struggling with mental health, please know that you aren't alone. Live your story. If you're in the process of healing yourself, live your story. If you struggle to be who you were created to be and are instead trying to live out who others think you should be, remember to live *your* story.

We don't get to choose who lives, who dies, and who tells our story, but we *can* control the storyline. Look in the mirror each day and know that there is no one else like you on this planet. You are one-of-a-kind and a chosen treasure of God on High. Your story matters.

Dream, see, write, live your story
Every day it keeps unfolding
Make it your own
The power is all yours [52]

---

[52] Parol, Tina. *Dream Big, Princess*. Walt Disney Records, 2018

You are not alone. If you or someone you know is in crisis, whether they are considering suicide or not, please call the toll-free National Suicide Lifeline at 800-273-TALK (8255) to speak with a trained crisis counselor.

If you don't want to talk on the phone, you can also text. Crisis Text Line offers free mental health support. Just text "10-18" or "SCRUBS" to 741741 for help.

The call and text lines are open 24 hours a day.

Appendix: Interview

Throughout this book, I've frequently stated that mental illness affects everyone. I would like to share an interview I recently did with friends of mine who have been dealing with their son's battle with mental illness. He has been struggling for many years. He experiences violent episodes but then doesn't remember the things he does. Keep in mind that these are parents who are trying to help their adult son, so for the sake of privacy, I'll just refer to them as John and Jane Doe.

Me: "Well, thank you both for sitting down to speak with me on this topic. I felt as though it was important for people to hear your story because it's quite a bit different from mine, and yet, we both have had struggles navigating this world of mental health."

John: "Navigating implies that we have a map and a destination."

Jane: "That's right, there is no map. The only thing I have figured out is how to get an appointment, but that comes after a month of calling place to place. I finally got that appointment, but the first available wasn't until April."

Me: "April? But you started calling around when?"

Jane: "It started in November and then everything went down late November into December and I started calling around for an appointment in January."

Me: "So the soonest you could get an appointment was four months after he was released from the mental health hospital?"

John: "Correct. We've had to feel our way through, though. Getting ten doors shut in our face. Getting ten people to tell you to do this, call this one, then call that one, but no one knows what that person does, so when you're done, call us back."

Jane: "The insurance companies have case management and I talked to a case manager one time. Now, they will send plenty of letters but they won't do any actual work. And I asked them, 'What am I supposed to be doing during this? There's no treatment right now between him getting released and his appointment.' But nobody ever has an answer for that."

John: "The one discharge psychologist wasn't even helpful. We sat there together as a family and she just asked us what we wanted to talk about. I'm sitting there and I'm like, 'You're the professional so I am going to defer to you.' And she told me that wasn't the way that it worked. She would let us talk to our son, and him to us, and she would just listen. I can do that at home and it wouldn't cost me a dime. And when he *would* talk, she wouldn't challenge anything he said no matter how off the wall it may have sounded. For us, it felt like a complete waste of time and money."

Me: "Is he currently on any type of medication?"

Jane: "Yes, he is, and he has enough refills until we get to finally see someone. We just hope that it's the right medication and that he doesn't have a relapse. We try to be very careful about what we say and what we do in the meantime around him. By the way, you can't Google how to do this and what to do."

Me: "So basically this has affected the entire family?"

John: "Yes, it has."

Jane: "It has. He's given us trauma. He's put us on edge and we don't know how that is going to manifest the next time he tries to threaten us unbeknownst to him. We are all very hypersensitive to his behavior. And it's stressful. I have asked him to tell us when he starts to feel the same as he did before because the police might not take him to the hospital the next time; they could send him to jail instead. And not only that, but it has also affected me as his mom. I mean, I'm driving him all over trying to find a hospital that will take him, and now I'm having a panic attack. What happens to the family who now develops mental health issues because we are trying to help our son with mental health issues? I'm developing anxiety issues. I've never had a panic attack before and there I was, on the side of the road having one."

Me: "What do you hope to get when it comes to mental health in this country?"

Jane: "A clear path, just like we have for cancer, diabetes, and other illnesses. Because when I went to my general practitioner and I had high blood pressure, he sent me to a cardiologist. I go to the cardiologist and he does tests, those tests come back to my doctor and me, and then we have a plan going forward. And I don't have to wait four months to get an appointment."

John: "I just hope that if there *is* a mental health crisis, immediate mental healthcare is available instead of: 'Well, let's throw them over here and medicate them and send them along their way.' We went to four different hospitals with our son, *nothing* constituted an emergency to get him care. Then we went to *five* different hospitals *with the police*, and we *still* couldn't get any help because they asked him, 'How are you doing?' and he said, 'Oh fine.' And they just sent him on home! We wouldn't be here with the police for no reason."

Jane: "And I would hope there was a place to go, because there may come a time when we have to say, 'No more.' But then where will he go? And will they let him in? A lot of people never make it to a place that can help them. The frustrating part is that urgent care never carries over to mental health. If I have an addiction, it's easy for me to go to a facility and be checked in, but that isn't always the case for mental health."

John: "Yeah, because in some cases they don't even know they *need* the help. I worry that one day I'm going to have to hurt my son because he doesn't know what he's doing. But why does it have to get to that point?"

Bibliography

Bishop, Alona. *How to Forgive Yourself: A Step-by-Step Guide to Forgiving Yourself and Letting Go of the Past.* CreateSpace Independent Publishing, 2015.

Groeschel, Craig. *Hope in the Dark: Believing God Is Good When Life Is Not.* Zondervan, 2018.

Kabat-Zinn, Jon. *Wherever You Go, There You Are: Mindfulness Meditation in Everyday Life.* Hachette Books, 2010.

Neff, Kristin. *Self-Compassion: The Proven Power of Being Kind to Yourself.* Yellow Kite, 2011.

Pueblo, Yung. *Clarity & Connection.* Andrews McMeel Publishing, 2021.

Salzberg, Sharon. *The Force of Kindness: Change Your Life with Love and Compassion.* Sounds True, 2010.

Shetty, Jay. *Think Like a Monk: Train Your Mind for Peace and Purpose Every Day.* Simon & Schuster, 2020.

White, Rozella Haydée. *Love Big: The Power of Revolutionary Relationships to Heal the World.* Fortress Press, 2019.

Williams, Michael. *Zen: Beginner's Guide to Understanding & Practicing Zen Meditation to Become Present.* 2017.

Printed in the United States
by Baker & Taylor Publisher Services